BASEBALL ALL-STARS:
TODAY'S GREATEST PLAYERS

Alan Schwarz

This Library Edition First Published and Exclusively Distributed by
The Rosen Publishing Group, Inc.
New York

This library edition first published in 2003 and exclusively distributed by
The Rosen Publishing Group, Inc., New York

Copyright © 2003 SPORTS ILLUSTRATED FOR KIDS Books

Book Design: Michelle Innes
Additional editorial material: Nel Yomtov

Photo Credits: Cover (left) pp. 23, 73, 86 © John Biever/SI/Icon SMI; cover (center), pp. 28, 66, 69, 87, 95 © Chuck Solomon/SI/Icon SMI; cover (right), pp. 8, 36, 54, 83 © John Iacono/SI/Icon SMI; pp. 12, 51 © ALLSPORT; pp. 14, 20, 85, 88, 89, 93, 97 © David Seelig/Icon SMI; p. 17 © Scott Wachter/Icon SMI; pp. 26, 78 © John Cordes/Icon SMI; pp. 31, 33 © Robert Beck/SI/Icon SMI; pp. 39, 100 © VJ Lovero/Icon SMI; pp. 44, 47, 57, 60, 82, 84 © Gary Rothstein/Icon SMI; pp. 64, 92 © Jason Wise/Icon SMI; p. 94 © Jim Gund/Icon SMI; p. 96 © Jeff Carlick/Icon SMI; p. 98 © Icon Sports Media; p. 101 © John McDonough/Icon SMI

First Edition

Library of Congress Cataloging-in-Publication Data

Schwarz, Alan.
  Baseball all-stars : today's greatest players / Alan Schwarz.-- 1st ed.
       p. cm.
"Sports illustrated for kids books."
Summary: Presents biographical and statistical information about some of the best baseball players.
 ISBN: 978-1-4358-8938-5
 1. Baseball players--Biography--Juvenile literature. 2. Baseball players--Rating of--Juvenile literature. [1. Baseball players.] I. Title.
 GV865.A1 S334 2003
 796.357'092'2--dc21

2002005916

>> CONTENTS

INTRODUCTION	4
AMERICAN LEAGUE (A.L.) STARTING LINEUP	6
A.L. PLAYERS	8
NATIONAL LEAGUE (N.L.) STARTING LINEUP	42
N.L. PLAYERS	44
HONORABLE MENTIONS	81
STARS OF THE FUTURE	91
TRIBUTES	99
MVP AWARD WINNERS	102
ROOKIE OF THE YEAR AWARD WINNERS	105
GLOSSARY	107
RESOURCES	108
INDEX	111

BASEBALL

» INTRODUCTION

Big-league baseball is full of big-time stars. There are veteran performers, young guns, and World Series wonders. There are home-team heroes and colorful characters from across the country. With so many stars, it's not always easy to say who's best. And that's where *we* come in.

Baseball All-Stars: Today's Greatest Players is your guide to the very best players in baseball. We've looked at each league, American and National, and selected the top player at each position. It wasn't easy! We picked some players, such as pitchers Pedro Martinez and Randy Johnson, because they're simply overpowering. We chose others, such as Ivan "Pudge" Rodriguez and Roberto Alomar, because they are defensive wizards.

We've even saved some space for Honorable Mentions, the athletes who didn't quite make our starting lineup. *Baseball All-Stars* includes the names

Introduction

you know, like veteran super-sluggers Barry Bonds and Sammy Sosa, as well as the game's rising young players. Check out these new faces in our Stars of the Future chapter. And in our Tributes chapter you can read about a pair of baseball legends — Cal Ripken, Jr. and Tony Gwynn.

As you can see, this book has more star power than most galaxies. So read on to find out which ones shine the brightest, and why we think these 40 men deserve to be called *Baseball All-Stars*.

BASEBALL ALL-STARS

>> AMERICAN LEAGUE

STARTING LINEUP

PEDRO MARTINEZ
RIGHT-HANDED PITCHER BOSTON RED SOX

BARRY ZITO
LEFT-HANDED PITCHER OAKLAND ATHLETICS

MARIANO RIVERA
RELIEF PITCHER NEW YORK YANKEES

IVAN RODRIGUEZ
CATCHER TEXAS RANGERS

JASON GIAMBI
FIRST BASE NEW YORK YANKEES

BRET BOONE
SECOND BASE SEATTLE MARINERS

ERIC CHAVEZ
THIRD BASE OAKLAND ATHLETICS

ALEX RODRIGUEZ
SHORTSTOP TEXAS RANGERS

ICHIRO SUZUKI
OUTFIELD SEATTLE MARINERS

JUAN GONZALEZ
OUTFIELD TEXAS RANGERS

MANNY RAMIREZ
OUTFIELD BOSTON RED SOX

EDGAR MARTINEZ
DESIGNATED HITTER SEATTLE MARINERS

BASEBALL ALL-STARS

PEDRO MARTINEZ
RIGHT-HANDED PITCHER, BOSTON RED SOX

Height 5 feet 11 inches
Weight 180 lbs.
Bats Right
Throws Right
Birth Date October 25, 1971
Birthplace Manoguayabo, Dominican Republic
Entered Majors 1992

SCOUTING REPORT

Pedro is one of the game's top pitchers, with an assortment of pitches that drive major league hitters crazy. He's got a fastball in the mid-90-miles-per-hour range, a great slider, a terrific change-up, and a fine curveball. Pedro has complete command over every pitch, possessing pinpoint control. Thanks to his athletic ability, he is also a solid fielder. He has a good pickoff move, too. Pedro has been known to tire as a long season wears on, and the Red Sox look to give him extra rest whenever they can.

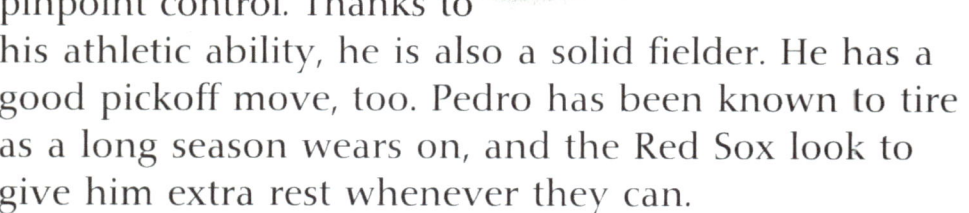

AMERICAN LEAGUE

A shoulder injury in 2001 limited Pedro to only 18 mound appearances. Everyone's eyes will be on this superstar hurler to see if he can return to dominance.

MAJOR LEAGUE CAREER

2001 After starting the year with a blistering 7-1 record and a 1.44 earned run average (ERA), Pedro went on the disabled list with a sore shoulder. He returned late in the year, but the velocity of his pitches was down. After three starts, he called it quits for the season. Even with the shoulder problem, which turned out to be a small tear in his rotator cuff, he held opposing batters to a measly .199 batting average. **2000** Pedro led the major leagues with a 1.74 ERA, and was second in strikeouts (284) and complete games (seven). He was unanimously selected for his third Cy Young Award, becoming the first pitcher in major league baseball history to unanimously win the award in three seasons. Pedro was also named the A.L. Pitcher of the Month for April with a 5-0 record and 1.27 ERA. **1999** Pedro won his second Cy Young Award. He led the majors in strikeouts (313) and led the A.L. with 23 wins. He was the starting pitcher at the All-Star Game at Fenway Park in Boston, where he struck out the first four batters he faced. For his performance, Pedro was named the All-Star Game MVP. He was also the A.L. Pitcher of the Month in April, May, June, and September. **1998** In his first season with the

BASEBALL ALL-STARS

FAST FACTS

> Has won three Cy Young Awards

> Has been selected to five All-Star teams (two with Montreal, three with Boston)

> Was the teammate of his older brother Ramon on the Red Sox in 1999 and 2000

Red Sox, Pedro won the A.L. MVP award and was named to the A.L. All-Star team. **1997** In his last season with the Montreal Expos, Pedro won his first Cy Young Award. He led the majors in ERA (1.90) and complete games (13). **1996** Pedro was selected to the N.L. All-Star team, and was third in the league with 222 strikeouts. He was selected to play with a group of major league All-Stars who toured Japan in the off-season. **1995** Pedro led the Expos with 14 wins and 174 strikeouts. He pitched nine perfect innings against the San Diego Padres, but lost the perfect game on a hit in the 10th inning by Bip Roberts. **1994** In his first full season as a Montreal Expo starter, Pedro went 11-5, winning his last five decisions. He had his first major league hit — a three-run triple against the Pittsburgh Pirates. Against the New York Mets, he also tossed his first career complete game and shutout. **1993** Pedro was used mostly in relief in his rookie year, leading N.L. relievers with 10 wins. He set a Los Angeles Dodger rookie record with 65 games pitched. **1992** Pedro spent most of the season in Albuquerque, New Mexico, with the Dodgers' Triple-A farm team, where he was 7-6 with a 3.81 ERA. He was selected to the AAA All-Star Game.

BARRY ZITO
LEFT-HANDED PITCHER, OAKLAND ATHLETICS

Height 6 feet 4 inches
Weight 215 lbs.
Bats Left
Throws Left
Birth Date May 13, 1978
Birthplace Las Vegas, Nevada
Entered Majors 2000

SCOUTING REPORT

Barry has one of the nastiest overhand curveballs in major league baseball. With a fastball that reaches about 90 miles per hour, and a very effective change–up, Barry makes things mighty tough on A.L. batters. He gets most of his outs on fly balls, but will continue to grow as a strikeout pitcher as he matures. Barry fields his position decently, and is still learning to hold base runners. Look for him to be the number one pitcher on the A's pitching staff.

AMERICAN LEAGUE

MAJOR LEAGUE CAREER

2001 Barry posted career bests in wins (17), innings pitched (214.1), strikeouts (205), shutouts (two), and starts (35). Barry was named the A.L.'s Pitcher of the Month in August and September, putting together a 9-1 record with a 1.14 ERA. He pitched a strong game against the Yankees in the playoff division series, holding the Bombers to only one run on two hits in eight innings. **2000** Barry went 7-4 with a 2.72 ERA in his rookie season. Barry was called up from Triple-A in Sacramento, California, on July 22 and made his major league debut later that day against the Anaheim Angels. Barry tied for third among A.L. rookies in strikeouts (78), tied for fourth in wins (seven), and was sixth in innings pitched (92.2). Barry was named A.L. Co-Player of the Week for the week of September 4, after going 2-0 without allowing a run in 15.2 innings.

FAST FACTS

> Held opposing batters to a .195 batting average in 2001

> Was the A's number one draft pick in 1999

> Attended the University of Southern California (USC), and as a junior, was selected first-team All-America by *USA Today*, *Baseball Weekly*, and *Baseball America*

MARIANO RIVERA
RELIEF PITCHER, NEW YORK YANKEES

Height 6 feet 2 inches
Weight 185 lbs.
Bats Right
Throws Right
Birth Date November 29, 1969
Birthplace Panama City, Panama
Entered Majors 1995

SCOUTING REPORT

Most baseball insiders say that Mariano is the best relief pitcher in the majors. Mariano isn't a big man, but his 97-mile-per-hour fastball gives both right-handed and left-handed batters huge problems. Mariano was at his best in 2001, thanks to the umpires' reinterpretation of the strike zone, which allowed for more high pitches to be called as strikes. Mariano allows few walks and few home runs. Despite his disappointing outing in Game 7 of the 2001 World Series *(see page 15)*, Mariano is the greatest post-season reliever of all time.

AMERICAN LEAGUE

MAJOR LEAGUE CAREER

2001 Only two outs away from another Yankee championship, Mariano blew a ninth-inning save against the Arizona Diamondbacks in Game 7 of the World Series. The Diamondbacks won the game, 4-3, and the World Series title. Even with the disappointment, Mariano had posted one of the best years of his career. He saved 50 games with a 2.34 ERA and 83 strikeouts in 80.2 innings pitched. He also held opponents to a lowly .209 batting average. Mariano was named to the A.L. All-Star team. **2000** Mariano was 7-4 with 36 saves in 66 appearances. He had three saves in the Yankees' World Series victory over the New York Mets. **1999** Mariano was 4-3 with a 1.83 ERA in 66 appearances. He led the A.L. in saves, save percentage (92 percent, saving 45 games in 49 chances) and relief ERA (1.83). Down the stretch, he did not allow a run in his final 28 appearances of the season (30.2 innings). He saved his last 22 save opportunities. Mariano was also named to his second All-Star Game. He was named Pitcher of the Month in August, notching 11 saves for the month. Mariano was named the World Series MVP, getting one win and two saves in the Yankees championship series over the Atlanta Braves. **1998** In his second year as the Yankees' closer, Mariano was 3-0 with a 1.91 ERA and 36 saves in 54 relief appearances. He saved three games for New York in their World Series win over the San Diego Padres. **1997** In his first season as Yankees' closer, Mariano established himself as one of

BASEBALL ALL-STARS

the top relievers in major league baseball. He went 6–4 with a 1.88 ERA and 43 saves in 66 relief appearances. He ranked second in the A.L. in ERA and saves. He ranked first in save opportunities (52) and sixth in games finished (56). Although he earned his first postseason save against the Cleveland Indians in the division series, he also blew a Game 4 save which allowed the Tribe to win the game and go on to win the series. **1996** Mariano was used primarily as a set-up man for Yankee closer John Wetteland. He was 8–3 with a 2.09 ERA and five saves in 61 appearances. Opponents hit just .189 against him. **1995** Mariano was called up from Triple-A in Columbus, Ohio and went 5–3 with a 5.54 ERA in 19 appearances with the Yanks. He made 10 starts with the Yankees, the only starts he made in his major league career.

FAST FACTS

> Mariano is 6–1 with a 0.91 ERA and 24 saves in 53 postseason appearances

> Only the third A.L. pitcher to save as many as 50 games in a season

AMERICAN LEAGUE

IVAN RODRIGUEZ
CATCHER, TEXAS RANGERS

Height 5 feet 9 inches
Weight 205 lbs.
Bats Right
Throws Right
Birth Date November 30, 1971
Birthplace Vega Baja, Puerto Rico
Entered Majors 1991

SCOUTING REPORT

Ivan is a free-swinger at the plate who can even hit pitches out of the strike zone very hard. With a .304 career batting average and a .485 slugging percentage, Ivan rates as one of baseball's all-time best offensive catchers. He has won 10 straight Gold Glove Awards. His strong arm makes him one of the most difficult catchers to run on in the majors. From 1998 to 2001, he threw out at least 50 percent of baserunners trying to steal.

BASEBALL ALL-STARS

MAJOR LEAGUE CAREER

2001 Ivan's season ended early because of an injury to his left knee. He played in only 111 games, and after improving his batting average in each of the previous four years, his mark slipped to .308. Ivan was selected to his 10th consecutive All-Star Game. **2000** Ivan's 27 home runs were the second-most in his career. **1999** Ivan hit 35 homers, a career high. He had two homers in a game five times. His 113 RBI's were also a personal best, as were his 25 stolen bases. **1998** Ivan knocked in more than 90 runs for the first time in his career (91). **1997** Ivan played in 150 games for the second straight season and tied a career high with 38 walks. **1996** Ivan had 639 plate appearances, a career high, and scored a career-high 116 runs. **1995** Ivan batted .300 for the first time in his career. **1994** Ivan became the first player to catch an

FAST FACTS

> Nickname is "Pudge"

> Donated $20,000 to the victims of the September 11, 2001, World Trade Center terrorist attacks

> Is the only Ranger to ever start in more than one All-Star Game

entire All-Star Game since Johnny Bench did it for the National League in 1975. Ivan won the first of his five Silver Slugger Awards. (A Silver Slugger Award is given to the best-hitting batter at each position. Both the N.L and the A.L. give the award.) **1993** Ivan made his first All-Star team at the age of 21. **1992** Ivan threw out 49 percent of runners attempting to steal on him. **1991** Ivan was called up from Triple-A in Tulsa, Oklahoma, on June 20, 1991, and started his first major league game that night.

BASEBALL ALL-STARS

JASON GIAMBI
FIRST BASEMAN, NEW YORK YANKEES

Height 6 feet 3 inches
Weight 235 lbs.
Bats Left
Throws Right
Birth Date January 8, 1971
Birthplace West Covina, California
Entered Majors 1995

SCOUTING REPORT

Jason is a dedicated professional, always looking to improve on his game. He has major-league power to all fields, but his .308 lifetime batting average shows that the long ball is not his only weapon. Jason is a solid clutch hitter who batted .397 with runners in scoring position in 2001. He's a fine defensive player and team leader, too. After signing a seven-year, $120 million contract with the Yankees, all eyes will be on Jason to see if he can put up the big numbers in New York.

AMERICAN LEAGUE

MAJOR LEAGUE CAREER

2001 Playing his last season for the Oakland A's, Jason led the A.L. in walks (129), doubles (47), slugging percentage (.660), and times on base (320). He tied for league lead in extra-base hits (87) and finished second in batting (.342). His batting average set an Oakland Athletics' single-season record. Jason helped lead the Athletics to the A.L. division series, which they lost to the New York Yankees, three games to two. Jason was named to his second straight All-Star Game and won his first Silver Slugger Award. **2000** Jason was named the A.L. MVP. He ranked among the Top 10 league leaders in home runs (43, tied for second), slugging percentage (.647, third), RBIs (137, tied for fourth), batting (.333, tied for seventh), total bases (330, eighth), and runs (108, tied for tenth). Jason was selected to his first All-Star team. **1999** Jason topped the A's in batting (.315), runs (115), hits (181), doubles (36), RBIs (123), and walks (105). He finished in the Top 10 in the league in walks, RBIs, on-base percentage, runs, and extra-base hits. **1998** Jason led the team in batting, home runs, and RBIs. He had hitting streaks of 17 and 16 games to become the first player in Oakland history to have two hitting streaks of more than 15 games in a single season. **1997** In his second full season in the majors, Jason broke his own club record for doubles with 41. **1996** Jason started games at five positions: left field, first base, third base, right field, and designated hitter.

BASEBALL ALL-STARS

1995 Jason made his major league debut on May 8, getting his first major league hit with an eighth inning single off Texas Ranger pitcher, Roger Pavlik.

FAST FACTS

> Drafted by the Milwaukee Brewers out of high school, but chose to go to college at Long Beach State University, in Long Beach, California

> Was a member of the bronze medal-winning U.S. baseball team at the 1991 Pan Am Games, in Havana, Cuba

> Was a member of the U.S. Olympic team that participated in Barcelona, Spain, in 1992

AMERICAN LEAGUE

BRET BOONE
SECOND BASEMAN, SEATTLE MARINERS

Height 5 feet 10 inches
Weight 190 lbs.
Bats Right
Throws Right
Birth Date April 6, 1969
Birthplace El Cajon, California
Entered Majors 1992

SCOUTING REPORT

Bret caught everyone's attention with a monster year at the plate in 2001. Never known for his power, Bret's off-season training program helped him add muscle to his frame, and he started to hit the ball to all parts of the field with tremendous power. Once a hitter who would most often hit to left field, Bret now drives the ball to right field, too. He's also a fine defensive player with a strong arm. Bret is solid at turning the double play and has better-than-average speed in the field. In addition, he's a smart baserunner who knows how to take the extra base when he can.

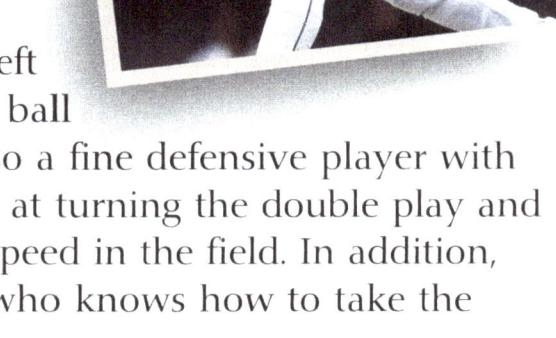

BASEBALL ALL-STARS

MAJOR LEAGUE CAREER

2001 In his second season with Seattle, Bret finished fourth in the A.L. in batting (.331) and knocked in a league-leading 141 runs. He totally crushed left-handed pitching, batting .444 with an astronomical .715 slugging percentage, ranking first among all A.L. batters. Bret was named the A.L.'s starting second baseman at the All-Star Game and won a Silver Slugger Award. **2000** In his first and only season with the San Diego Padres, Bret led the team with 19 homers and 74 RBIs, even though he played in only 127 games due to injuries. He became the first second baseman in major league history to have two three-home-run games in one season. **1999** Playing for the Atlanta Braves, Bret had career highs in plate appearances (608) with 102 runs scored and 14 stolen bases. In playoff and World Series action, Bret hit .370 in 14 games against the Houston Astros, New York Mets, and New York Yankees. **1998** Playing for the Cincinnati Reds, Bret was named to his first All-Star team and won his first Gold Glove Award. **1997** Bret tied a major league record for second basemen by leading the league in fielding for a third straight season. He set a major league record for second basemen with a .997 fielding percentage, making only two errors in 607 chances. After the season, his glove was sent to the Baseball Hall of Fame, in Cooperstown, New York. **1996** For the second straight year, Bret led N.L. second basemen with a .991 fielding percentage. **1995** Bret hit two home runs in the same game for the

AMERICAN LEAGUE

FAST FACTS

> Grandfather, Ray, played 13 years in the major leagues (1948–60) with the Indians, Tigers, White Sox, Athletics, Braves, and Red Sox

> Father, Bob, is the current manager of the Cincinnati Reds, and played 19 seasons (1972–90) with the Phillies, Angels, and Royals

> Brother, Aaron, currently plays for the Reds

> Named to his first All-Star team to replace the injured Sammy Sosa in 1998

first time in his career. He also took part in the only two triple plays made in the N.L. in 1995. Bret led N.L. second basemen with a .994 fielding percentage, making only four errors in 677 chances. **1994** Playing for the Cincinnati Reds in his first full season in the majors, Bret tied for eighth in the N.L. in batting average. **1993** In his second season with the Mariners, Bret was called up from Triple-A in Calgary, Alberta, Canada, and started 56 of the Mariners last 58 games. **1992** Bret made his major league debut with Seattle on August 19 against the Baltimore Orioles, and got his first hit in his first at-bat.

BASEBALL ALL-STARS

ERIC CHAVEZ
THIRD BASEMAN, OAKLAND ATHLETICS

Height 6 feet 1 inch
Weight 206 lbs.
Bats Left
Throws Right
Birth Date December 7, 1977
Birthplace Los Angeles, California
Entered Majors 1998

SCOUTING REPORT

Eric has established himself as one of baseball's premier third basemen. His power numbers are beginning to grow, and there's no telling how good of a long-ball hitter he will become. He hits the ball well into the gaps in left and right centerfield. Eric has good speed, and should be stealing in the range of 15–20 bases a season. Expect him to be scoring 100 runs a season regularly. Eric is a fabulous defensive fielder, making the fewest number of errors by an A.L. third baseman (12) in 2001. Look for him to hit 30 homers and knock in 100 runs a season for years to come.

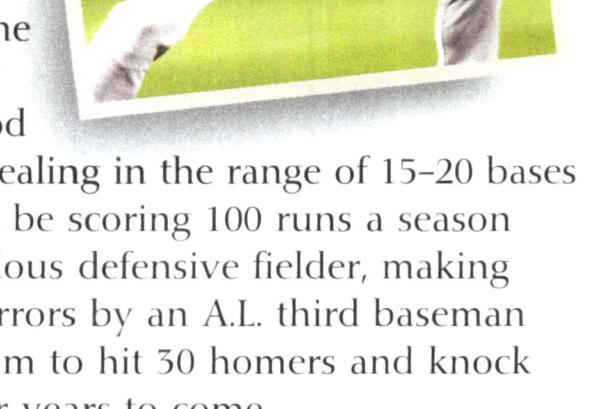

AMERICAN LEAGUE

MAJOR LEAGUE CAREER

2001 Eric had a breakout year, setting career highs in just about every offensive category. He finished fourth in the league in doubles (43), ninth in extra-base hits (75), and 10th in RBI's (114). Eric also won his first Gold Glove Award. **2000** Eric took over at third base when Olmedo Saenz went down with an injury. He finished third in home runs by an A.L. third baseman (26) behind the Angels' Troy Glaus (46) and the Blue Jays' Tony Batista (41). His .951 fielding percentage was seventh among A.L. third basemen. **1999** In his rookie season, Eric ranked seventh in home runs (13), eighth in RBI's (50) and extra-base hits (36), and 10th in total bases (152) among A.L. rookies. He batted .462 with six RBI's as a pinch hitter (six for 13). **1998** In a brief 45-at-bat stint in the big leagues, Eric batted .311 with six RBI's.

FAST FACTS

> Along with A's shortstop, Miguel Tejada, the pair became the first third baseman-shortstop duo to each hit 30 homers with 100 RBIs in the same season

> Was a two-time *Baseball America* High School All-America at Mount Carmel High School, in Los Angeles, California

> Drafted by the A's in the 1996 draft

BASEBALL ALL-STARS

ALEX RODRIGUEZ
SHORTSTOP, TEXAS RANGERS

Height 6 feet 3 inches
Weight 210 lbs.
Bats Right
Throws Right
Birth Date July 27, 1975
Birthplace New York, New York
Entered Majors 1994

SCOUTING REPORT

Alex is quite possibly the greatest shortstop ever to play in the major leagues. He's an outstanding player who can do it all — hit, hit with power, run, throw, and field. Alex owns a lifetime .311 batting average — and now playing in the hitter-friendly Arlington Stadium  in Houston, Texas, he's a legitimate threat to win a Triple Crown (leading the league in home runs, RBI's and batting average). He's a brilliant baserunner when stealing or going for the extra base. Alex has great range in the field because of his size and he possesses a strong throwing arm.

AMERICAN LEAGUE

After signing a $252-million contract with the Rangers before the start of the 2001 season, Alex's numbers are proving to everyone that he was worth the money.

MAJOR LEAGUE CAREER

2001 Alex's first season in a Rangers uniform was one of the best offensive showings ever by a shortstop. He led the A.L. with 52 homers, 133 runs scored, 87 extra-base hits, and 393 total bases. His 52 home runs set the all-time major league record for most by a shortstop, breaking Ernie Banks's mark of 47 in 1958. He was named to the All-Star team for the fifth time in his career and won his fifth Silver Slugger Award. **2000** Playing in his last season with the Seattle Mariners, Alex was second in the league in runs scored (134) and led the team in runs, total bases, homers, and sacrifice flies. He also set a career high for most walks (100). Alex picked up his fourth Silver Slugger Award. **1999** Alex missed 32 games due to a knee injury, but finished fifth in the A.L. in homers (42). He was second on the Mariners in runs (110), total bases (294), and RBIs (111). He won his third Silver Slugger Award. **1998** Alex led the league in at-bats (686), hits (213), and multi-hit games (64). He was named to his second All-Star team and he won his second Silver Slugger Award. With 42 homers and 46 stolen bases, Alex became only the third player in major league history with 40 homers and 40 steals in a single season (Jose Canseco in 1988 and Barry Bonds in 1996 were the others).

BASEBALL ALL-STARS

1997 Alex started 140 games at short, while leading the Mariners in doubles (40) and ranking third in hits (176) and total bases (291). **1996** In his first full major league season, Alex led the A.L. in batting (.358), runs scored (141), total bases (379), and doubles (54). He placed second in the league in hits (215) and extra base hits (91). Alex was the A.L. Player of the Month in August. He also won his first Silver Slugger Award. **1995** Alex was up and down between Seattle and the minors, making four separate trips to the big leagues. He hit his first major league homer off the Kansas City Royals' Tom Gordon on June 12. **1994** Alex made his major league debut on June 8 in Boston. He was 18 years, 11 months, and 11 days old. He played 17 games for Seattle and was sent back to the minors for the rest of the season.

FAST FACTS

> Holds Rangers' single-season records for home runs, runs scored, total bases, and hit by pitches; second most extra-base hits, and fourth highest RBI total

> Is the 2002 national spokesperson for Boys and Girls Clubs of America

> Selected as the USA Baseball Junior Player of the Year and as Gatorade's National Baseball Student Athlete of the Year, as a senior at Westminster Christian High School in Miami, Florida

AMERICAN LEAGUE

ICHIRO SUZUKI
OUTFIELDER, SEATTLE MARINERS

Height 5 feet 9 inches
Weight 160 lbs.
Bats Left
Throws Right
Birth Date October 22, 1973
Birthplace Kasugai, Japan
Entered Majors 2001

SCOUTING REPORT

Despite some pre-season criticism from people who thought he would not be able to handle hard-throwing pitchers in the United States, Ichiro had one of the greatest rookie seasons of all time in 2001. His short, quick stroke allows him to shoot the ball through holes in the infield or drive the ball into the outfield gaps. His unique stride into the ball just before making contact is actually his first step toward first base — giving him a "running start" down the line. Ichiro doesn't walk much, but because he's such a good contact hitter, he doesn't

BASEBALL ALL-STARS

strike out much, either — only 53 times in 692 at-bats. Ichiro's great range, strong throwing arm, and soft hands help make him one of the top defensive outfielders in the league. He's a great basestealer and will run in almost any situation. Ichiro will have many productive seasons in the future.

MAJOR LEAGUE CAREER

2001 Ichiro led the majors in batting average (.350) and stolen bases (56), becoming the first player to do so since Jackie Robinson in 1949. His major league-leading 242 hits and 692 at-bats set A.L. rookie records. Ichiro was second in the A.L. in runs scored (127) and ninth in total bases (316). His 192 singles set a major league rookie record. In this blockbuster season, Ichiro won Rookie of the Year, was named to the All-Star team, won a Gold Glove award, and won the A.L. MVP Award.

FAST FACTS

> Played nine years with the Orix Blue Wave in Japan's Pacific League

> Led the Pacific League in batting average for seven straight seasons, from 1994–2000

> Won three MVP awards and seven consecutive Gold Gloves while playing in Japan

AMERICAN LEAGUE

JUAN GONZALEZ
OUTFIELDER, TEXAS RANGERS

Height 6 feet 3 inches
Weight 220 lbs.
Bats Right
Throws Right
Birth Date October 16, 1969
Birthplace Vega Baja, Puerto Rico
Entered Majors 1989

SCOUTING REPORT

Juan is a dangerous batter who can take any pitcher deep on a fastball or inside curve. He's an RBI machine, having knocked it at least 100 RBIs eight times in his career. Before knee and hamstring problems slowed him down, Juan was a very good baserunner, always looking for the extra base. He has a strong, accurate throwing arm and shows good range in the field.

MAJOR LEAGUE CAREER

2001 In his one season with the Cleveland Indians, Juan led the A.L. in sacrifice flies (16), was second in RBIs (140), fifth in slugging percentage (.590), and sixth in batting (.325). He topped the Indians in RBIs and slugging, and was second in average, at-bats, hits, and total bases. He was named to his third All-Star team and won his sixth Silver Slugger Award. **2000** Back injuries limited Juan to only 115 games in his only season with the Detroit Tigers. He had his lowest batting average and homer total since 1994, and his fewest number of RBIs in a full season. **1999** With the Texas Rangers, Juan batted a career-high .326 and drew a career-high 51 walks. He finished fifth in the league in RBIs (128), fourth in slugging (.601), and sixth in total bases (338). **1998** Juan won his second A.L. MVP Award, finishing second in the majors in RBIs (157) and extra base hits (97). He led the league in doubles (50). Juan earned his fifth Silver Slugger Award. **1997** Juan finished third in the A.L. in home runs (42) and RBIs (131) even though he missed 29 games because of injuries. He was the A.L. Player of the Month for September. **1996** Juan won his first MVP Award, ranking second in the league in RBIs (144) and slugging (.643). He was selected as the league Player of the Month for July. **1995** Playing only 90 games due to injuries, Juan still finished second on the Rangers in homers (27) and RBIs (82). **1994** Juan hit only 19 homers,

AMERICAN LEAGUE

the fewest number in his career in a full season. **1993** Juan tied for the major league lead in homers (46), while topping the A.L. in slugging (.632) and ranking second in total bases (339). He set club records at the time for homers, slugging, and extra base hits. Juan made his first All-Star team. **1992** Juan led the majors in homers (43), ranked third in the A.L. in total bases (309), and ranked fourth in extra-base hits (69). **1991** Juan led the Rangers in homers (27) and was second in RBIs (102). **1990** Juan saw action in 25 games during the season, after winning the MVP Award at his minor league club of Oklahoma City, Oklahoma, in the American Association. **1989** Juan appeared in 24 games.

FAST FACTS

> Drove in 1,161 runs (from 1991–2001), the most of any major league player during that time

> Hit eight home runs with 15 RBIs in 15 postseason games

> Selected as 1997 Texas Rangers Roberto Clemente Man of the Year for community achievement

BASEBALL ALL-STARS

MANNY RAMIREZ
OUTFIELDER, BOSTON RED SOX

Height 6 feet
Weight 213 lbs.
Birth Date May 30, 1972
Birthplace Santo Domingo, Dominican Republic
Bats Right
Throws Right
Entered Majors 1993

SCOUTING REPORT

Manny is possibly the best hitter is baseball. He has great power to all fields and is an extremely tough out with men on base. There's no telling how many homers Manny will hit in Boston's Fenway Park with its short distance down the left field line. He is not a fast baserunner and rarely tries to steal bases. In the outfield, he is an average fielder with a fair throwing arm.

AMERICAN LEAGUE

MAJOR LEAGUE CAREER

2001 Playing in his first season with the Red Sox, Manny was selected to his fifth All-Star team. He finished the season tied for fourth in the league in homers (41) and sixth in total bases (322). Manny won his third Silver Slugger Award. **2000** In his last season with the Cleveland Indians, Manny hit a career-high .351 with 38 homers and 122 RBIs in only 118 games. Hamstring injuries kept him out of 44 games. He made the All-Star team for the fourth time. **1999** Manny set an Indians' record for most RBIs in a season with 165. His 44 home runs were the fourth most ever hit by an Indian. He won his second Silver Slugger Award and made the All-Star team for the third time. **1998** Manny was named the Indians' Man of the Year after hitting a career-high 45 home runs. He made his second A.L. All-Star team. **1997** Manny's .328 batting average tied for fourth in the A.L. He also hit three grand slams. **1996** Manny had his second straight 30-homer, 100-RBI season. He also hit three grand slams, the first Indian to do it since Andre Thornton in 1979. Manny led A.L. outfielders with 19 assists. **1995** In his first big season, Manny won his first Silver Slugger Award and was named to his first All-Star team. He was named A.L. Player of the Month for May when he hit .394 with 11 homers and 27 RBIs. **1994** Manny finished second in the voting for A.L. Rookie of the Year to

BASEBALL ALL-STARS

Kansas City Royal Bob Hamelin. He was second among A.L. rookies in many categories including hits, doubles, home runs, and RBIs. **1993** Manny got his first major league hit, a double. In the same game, he hit his first major league home run.

FAST FACTS

> His 13 career grand slams hit as a Cleveland Indian are a team record

> His 557 RBIs from 1998–2001 are second only to Sammy Sosa's 597 RBIs

> Was the New York City Public School's High School Player of the Year in 1991

AMERICAN LEAGUE

EDGAR MARTINEZ
DESIGNATED HITTER, SEATTLE MARINERS

Height 5 feet 11 inches
Weight 210 lbs.
Birth Date January 2, 1963
Birthplace New York, New York
Bats Right
Throws Right
Entered Majors 1987

SCOUTING REPORT

Edgar's patience at the plate has made him the greatest designated hitter of all time. He has power to all fields, and even when pitchers try to move him off the plate by pitching Edgar inside, he can still stroke the ball with authority. Edgar came up to the big leagues as a third baseman, but became a full-time DH in 1995. One of the reasons for the switch was the number of muscle problems he experienced in his legs. Because of that, Edgar doesn't try to steal much, and he's not a threat to go for the extra base.

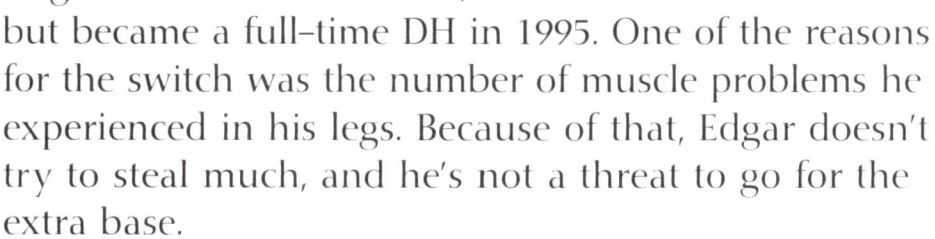

BASEBALL

MAJOR LEAGUE CAREER

2001 Edgar was named Designated Hitter of the Year, hitting over .300 for the 11th time in his career, and driving in 100 runs for the sixth time. He was named to his sixth All-Star team and won his fifth Silver Slugger Award. **2000** Edgar had his greatest season ever, leading the league with a career-high 145 RBIs. His RBI total set a major league record for most by a player 37 years old or older. He also hit a career-high 37 homers. Edgar was named A.L. Player of the Month for May after batting .441 with 10 homers and 42 runs knocked in. He was named to his fifth All-Star team. **1999** Edgar had a monster second half, batting .360 after the All-Star break. He was fourth in the A.L. in batting (.337) and seventh in walks (97). **1998** Edgar was named Outstanding Designated Hitter of the A.L. He finished second in the league in doubles (46), third in walks (106), and batting average (.322). **1997** Edgar finished second in the league with a .330 batting average and was voted Outstanding Designated Hitter. In interleague play, he hit a blistering .475 with seven homers and 14 RBIs in just 40 at-bats. He was named to his fourth All-Star team. **1996** Despite missing 21 days on the disabled list, Edgar was named to his third All-Star team. **1995** Edgar won his second straight batting title (.356). It was the highest average by an A.L. right-handed hitter since Joe DiMaggio hit .381 in 1939. He was selected to his second All-Star Game, won a

Silver Slugger Award, and was named Outstanding Designated Hitter. **1994** Edgar played in only 89 games due to wrist injuries. **1993** Edgar was slowed down by leg injuries, playing in only 42 games. **1992** Edgar won his first batting title, the first one in Mariners' team history. He tied for the league in doubles (46), ranked second in slugging (.544), and fifth in extra-base hits (67). He was named the Player of the Month in August. Edgar was also named to his first All-Star team and won his first Silver Slugger Award. **1991** Edgar finished fifth in the league in on-base percentage (.405). **1990** In his first full season in the majors, Edgar finished sixth in the league with a .302 batting average. **1989** Edgar started the season as the Mariners' third baseman. He was sent back to the minors, brought back up to Seattle, and then sent back to the minors. **1988** and **1987** Edgar played briefly in Seattle, getting a total of only 75 at-bats. He batted a combined .333 in the two seasons.

> Has hit over .300 ten times in his career

> Owns an embroidery company in Redmond, Washington

BASEBALL ALL-STARS

>> NATIONAL LEAGUE

STARTING LINEUP

CURT SCHILLING
RIGHT-HANDED PITCHER **ARIZONA DIAMONDBACKS**

RANDY JOHNSON
LEFT-HANDED PITCHER **ARIZONA DIAMONDBACKS**

TREVOR HOFFMAN
RELIEF PITCHER **SAN DIEGO PADRES**

MIKE PIAZZA
CATCHER **NEW YORK METS**

JEFF BAGWELL
FIRST BASE HOUSTON ASTROS

ROBERTO ALOMAR
SECOND BASE NEW YORK METS

PLACIDO POLANCO
THIRD BASE ST. LOUIS CARDINALS

RICH AURILIA
SHORTSTOP SAN FRANCISCO GIANTS

SAMMY SOSA
OUTFIELD CHICAGO CUBS

BARRY BONDS
OUTFIELD SAN FRANCISCO GIANTS

LARRY WALKER
OUTFIELD COLORADO ROCKIES

BASEBALL

CURT SCHILLING
RIGHT-HANDED PITCHER, ARIZONA DIAMONDBACKS

Height 6 feet 5 inches
Weight 235 lbs.
Birth Date November 14, 1966
Birthplace Anchorage, Alaska
Bats Right
Throws Right
Entered Majors 1988

SCOUTING REPORT

Curt has great control on all of his pitches. He has one of the best fastballs in the league, a tough split-finger, a good slider, and a tough-to-handle overhand curve. Because of his terrific control, Curt allows a lot of home runs. At the plate, Curt is a good bunter, but is not a good hitter. He's a solid fielder, and with his quick delivery to the plate, it's tough for base runners to steal on him. Curt is a true professional, who dedicates a lot of time to conditioning and preparation.

NATIONAL LEAGUE

MAJOR LEAGUE CAREER

2001 Curt helped lead the Diamondbacks to their first World Series title against the New York Yankees. In six postseason games, he posted a 4-0 record and struck out 56 batters in 48.1 innings with a 1.12 ERA. He was named co-winner of the World Series MVP, along with teammate Randy Johnson. During the season, Curt led the league in wins (22), innings pitched (256.2), and complete games (six). Curt also was second in the league in ERA (2.98) and strikeouts (293). Curt finished second to Randy in the voting for the N.L. Cy Young Award. He was named to his fourth All-Star team. **2000** Curt started the season with the Philadelphia Phillies, with whom he went 6-6. He finished the season with the D-Backs, appearing in 13 games, while posting a 5-6 record. He led the league in complete games with eight. **1999** Curt was named to his third All-Star Game. **1998** Curt led the N.L. in innings pitched (268.2) and strikeouts (300). He made the N.L. All-Star team for the second time. **1997** Curt led the N.L. in strikeouts with 319 and was fifth in the league with 17 wins. He made his first All-Star team. **1996** Curt led the league with eight complete games. **1995** Curt led the Phillies with 114 strikeouts. **1994** Curt was the number four starting pitcher, winning only two games. **1993** Curt tied for the team lead in wins (16) with Tommy Greene. He led Phils' pitchers in innings pitched (235.1) and strikeouts (186). Curt was the MVP of the N.L. Championship Series against the Atlanta Braves. In the series, he struck out 19 batters in 16 innings and posted a 1.69 ERA. **1992** In his first season with the Phillies, Curt led the team in wins (14) and strikeouts (147). **1991** In his only season with the Houston Astros, Curt was used exclusively as a reliever, saving eight games. **1990** In his final season with the Baltimore Orioles, Curt saved three games. **1989** Curt appeared in only five games, making one start. **1988** Curt started four games and lost three of them.

FAST FACTS

> Has led league in strikeouts twice, innings pitched twice, and complete games four times

> Is a World War II history buff

NATIONAL LEAGUE

RANDY JOHNSON
LEFT-HANDED PITCHER, ARIZONA DIAMONDBACKS

Height 6 feet 10 inches
Weight 235 lbs.
Birth Date September 10, 1963
Birthplace Walnut Creek, California
Bats Right
Throws Left
Entered Majors 1988

SCOUTING REPORT

Randy is one of the most dominating pitchers of all time. He has won four Cy Young Awards and has led the league in strikeouts seven times. Randy's big weapon is a fastball that can exceed 100 miles per hour. He's also got a nasty slider that breaks away from left-handed batters 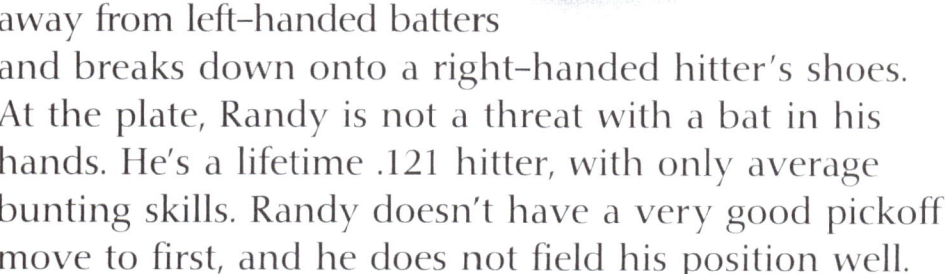 and breaks down onto a right-handed hitter's shoes. At the plate, Randy is not a threat with a bat in his hands. He's a lifetime .121 hitter, with only average bunting skills. Randy doesn't have a very good pickoff move to first, and he does not field his position well.

He has a tendency to hurry his throws when trying to throw out base runners. Still, Randy, close to 40 years old, is a workhorse capable of pitching 225–260 innings a year and will probably do so for at least two or three more seasons.

MAJOR LEAGUE CAREER

2001 Randy had another monster season, winning his third straight Cy Young Award, and fourth of his career. He won a career-high 21 games and led the majors in strikeouts (372) for the seventh time in his career. His strikeout total was also the best of his career. Randy's ERA of 2.49 earned him his second ERA title in the last three years. Randy was named to the 2001 All-Star team, too. He was virtually unhittable in the playoffs and went 5-1 against the Cardinals in the N.L. division series, the Braves in the league championship series, and the Yankees in the World Series. He won three games in the Series and was named co-MVP of the World Series with teammate Curt Schilling. **2000** Randy won his second straight Cy Young Award, leading the majors with 347 strikeouts. He led the N.L. in winning percentage (.731), and tied for the league's top spot in complete games (eight), shutouts (three), and starts (35). He was the Pitcher of the Month for April, going 6-0. Randy was named to the All-Star team. **1999** In his first season with the Diamondbacks, Randy earned his second Cy Young Award. He led the

NATIONAL LEAGUE

league in ERA (2.48), strikeouts (364), and complete games (12). He was also named to the All-Star team. **1998** After 10 seasons in Seattle, Randy was traded to the Houston Astros during the season. He was only 9-10 with the Mariners, but turned things around and posted a brilliant 10-1 record with a 1.28 ERA with the Astros. He threw four shutouts in his brief stint in Houston. **1997** Randy had his first 20-win season, while ranking second in the league in ERA (2.28), strikeouts (291), and wins. He finished second to Toronto's Roger Clemens in the Cy Young voting. Randy was the starting pitcher for the A.L. All-Star team. **1996** A serious back injury limited Randy to only 14 games, but he won all five of his decisions. **1995** Randy won his first Cy Young Award. He led the league in ERA (2.48) and strikeouts (294). He was named to the All-Star team for the fourth time. **1994** Randy led the majors with 204 strikeouts, and led the A.L. in complete games (nine) and shutouts (four). He was named to the A.L. All-Star team. **1993** Randy led the majors for the second straight year with 308 strikeouts. He made his second All-Star team. **1992** Randy had a career-longest losing streak of eight games, but he led the league with 241 strikeouts. **1991** Battling serious back problems, Randy was still able to finish second in the league in strikeouts (228). **1990** Randy pitched the first no-hitter in Mariners' history against the Detroit Tigers, on June 2. He was the A.L. Pitcher of the Month for June, going 5-0 with a 2.40 ERA. Randy was named to his first All-Star team. **1989** Randy began the season with the Montreal Expos, going 0-4 with a 6.67 ERA. He was sent to Triple-A in Indianapolis, Indiana, and then traded to the Mariners on May 25. **1988** Randy spent most of the season in Triple-A in Indianapolis, Indiana, but was called up to the big leagues by the Expos and won his major league debut on September 15 against the Pittsburgh Pirates.

FAST FACTS

> Has struck out 300 or more batters in five seasons

> Only the fourth pitcher to win at least four Cy Young Awards (Gregg Maddux, Steve Carlton, and Roger Clemens are the others)

> Hobbies include playing the drums and photography

TREVOR HOFFMAN
RELIEF PITCHER, SAN DIEGO PADRES

Height 6 feet
Weight 215 lbs.
Birth Date October 13, 1967
Birthplace Bellflower, California
Bats Right
Throws Right
Entered Majors 1993

SCOUTING REPORT

Trevor mixes a straight change-up with a blazing fastball in the mid-90-miles-per-hour range. He can work on several straight days without losing his ability to retire batters. As a reliever, Trevor doesn't get to the plate much, and he's only a .121 career hitter in 33 at-bats. Trevor has been one of the most durable relief pitchers of the 1990s, and just when you think he's slowing down, he saves 43 of 46 opportunities, as he did in 2001. If he stays healthy, he can remain effective for several more seasons.

BASEBALL ALL-STARS

FAST FACTS

> Is the only pitcher to have five seasons of 40 saves in a career

> Tied N.L. record for saves in one season with 53, in 1998

> One of his older brothers, Glenn, was a major league infielder from 1980–1989 and managed the Dodgers in 1998

MAJOR LEAGUE CAREER

2001 Trevor had his fifth career 40-save season, as he joined only 13 other major league pitchers in history to have 300 career saves. With his 43 saves, he became the first pitcher in baseball history to have five seasons of 40 saves, and the first to ever have four 40-save seasons in a row. **2000** Trevor was named to his third straight All-Star team and was second in the N.L. in saves, with 43. **1999** Trevor saved 40 of 43 opportunities, as he earned his second selection to the N.L. All-Star team. **1998** Trevor led the major leagues in saves with 53 and had a 1.48 ERA. He finished second in voting for the N.L. Cy Young Award, behind Atlanta's Tom Glavine, and was named to his first All-Star team. **1997** Trevor finished second in the

NATIONAL LEAGUE

league in saves with 37. **1996** Trevor's 42 saves was third-best in the National League and he led N.L. relievers in wins (nine) and strikeouts (111). **1995** Trevor led the Padres with 55 appearances and his 31 saves were sixth-best in the league. **1994** In his first full season with San Diego, Trevor notched his first 20-save season. **1993** Trevor started the year with the Florida Marlins, making 28 appearances. He was traded to the Padres and appeared in 39 games, going 2-4 with three saves.

BASEBALL ALL-STARS

MIKE PIAZZA
CATCHER, NEW YORK METS

Height 6 feet 3 inches
Weight 215 lbs.
Birth Date September 4, 1968
Birthplace Norristown, Pennsylvania
Bats Right
Throws Right
Entered Majors 1992

SCOUTING REPORT

Mike may be the greatest hitting catcher of all time. He has enormous power to all fields, capable of hitting skyscraping majestic blasts or laser-like line drives over the fences. On the bases, Mike hustles and runs aggressively, but his speed is slightly below average. Defensively, Mike usually ranks last in throwing out basestealers, but he blocks balls effectively and works well with the Mets' pitching staff. There's been talk of moving Mike to first base to save wear and tear

NATIONAL LEAGUE

on his body, but he currently remains behind the plate, playing the game with passion and a strong competitive spirit.

MAJOR LEAGUE CAREER

2001 Mike hit at least 30 home runs for the seventh straight season and batted .300 for the ninth straight full season, even though the Mets had a weak lineup to protect their big slugger. Mike made his ninth All-Star team and won his ninth straight Silver Slugger Award.

2000 Mike finished tenth in the N.L. in batting average (.324), tenth in home runs (38), and ninth in slugging percentage (.614). He led the majors with a .377 batting average on the road. Mike helped the Mets make it into the World Series for the first time since 1986. The Mets lost the series to the New York Yankees, four games to one.

1999 Mike became the first catcher ever to hit 40 homers in a season twice. Mike made the All-Star team and won a Silver Slugger Award. **1998** Mike finished fourth in the N.L. in batting (.328). He won his sixth straight Silver Slugger Award and was named to his sixth All-Star team. He hit his 200th career homer on September 16.

1997 Mike's .362 batting average was the highest ever by a catcher (playing in more than 110 games) in major league history, tying Bill Dickey who hit .362 in 1936. Mike won the N.L. Player of the Month Award twice. In July, he hit .431 with nine homers and 25 RBIs, and in August, he hit .320 with 10 homers and 27 RBIs. Mike

BASEBALL ALL-STARS

FAST FACTS

> Named to nine straight All-Star Games and won nine straight Silver Slugger Awards

> Named N.L. Rookie of the Year in 1993

> Enjoys playing the drums to relax

was an All-Star and Silver Slugger Award winner once again. **1996** Mike finished second in MVP voting behind Ken Caminiti of the San Diego Padres. He won his fourth Silver Slugger Award and was named the MVP of the All-Star Game, after hitting a double and a home run and knocking in two runs. **1995** Mike finished second in the league in batting (.346). He was named to the All-Star team and won another Silver Slugger Award. Mike was the Player of the Month in August with a .400 average, nine homers, and 25 RBIs. **1994** Mike made the All-Star team and won his second Silver Slugger Award. He was N.L. co-Player of the Month in May, after batting .386 with six home runs and 24 RBIs. **1993** Mike won the N.L. Rookie of the Year Award, was named to his first All-Star team and won his first Silver Slugger Award. **1992** Mike made his major league debut on September 1 and went three-for-three with a double and a walk against the Chicago Cubs.

NATIONAL LEAGUE

JEFF BAGWELL
FIRST BASEMAN, HOUSTON ASTROS

Height 6 feet
Weight 215 lbs.
Birth Date May 27, 1968
Birthplace Boston, Massachusetts
Bats Right
Throws Right
Entered Majors 1991

SCOUTING REPORT

Jeff has a huge, powerful uppercut in his swing. He hits to all fields with power. Although he strikes out well over 100 times a season, he has become a more selective hitter over the years, as shown by six straight seasons of 100+ walks. On the bases, Jeff is a good percentage base-stealer and knows when to take the extra base. He's a fine fielder, especially good on charging bunts and in scooping up grounders. Jeff shows no indication that he's slowing down. He has been the Opening Day first baseman for the Astros for 11 straight seasons. Jeff plays through aches and pains

BASEBALL ALL-STARS

and should continue to put up big power numbers at his home field, Astros Field, in Houston, Texas.

MAJOR LEAGUE CAREER

2001 His 130 RBIs made him the only Houston player to have 100+ RBIs in six straight seasons. He was the N.L. Player of the Month for July, hitting .333 with nine homers and 36 RBIs. **2000** Jeff finished third among league leaders in home runs (47), RBIs (132), and walks (107). Jeff scored 152 runs, breaking Craig Biggio's previous team record of 146 in 1997. He set a club record with 28 homers hit at home. **1999** Jeff set team records during the season for career home runs (263), RBIs (960), extra-base hits (598), and walks (878). He hit three home runs in a game twice, becoming only the 13th player in major league history to do so. Jeff was named to his fourth All-Star team and won his third Silver Slugger Award. **1998** Jeff hit his first career grand slam on September 8. He missed 15 games due to injuries. **1997** Jeff ranked among league leaders in runs (109, fifth), doubles (40, seventh), slugging percentage (.592, third), and total bases (335, fourth). He was named to his third All-Star team and won his second Silver Slugger Award. **1996** Jeff was once again among league leaders in batting (.315, eighth), RBIs (120, sixth), extra-base hits (81, fourth), and slugging percentage (.570, sixth). He was named to the All-Star team for the second time. **1995** Jeff finished the season on a hot streak, hitting 16 homers and knocking in 70 runs in the final 78 games. **1994** Jeff won the N.L. MVP Award, as he

NATIONAL LEAGUE

FAST FACTS

> Only the eighth player in major league history to have six straight 30+ home run and 100+ RBI seasons

> Only the second N.L. player to have 300 homers, 1,000 RBIs, 1,000 runs, and 1,000 walks in his first 11 major league seasons (Eddie Matthews is the other, doing it from 1952-62)

> Selected by the Boston Red Sox in the June 1989 draft after playing three years at the University of Hartford, in Connecticut

became the first player to finish first or second in the National League in batting average, runs, RBIs, and homers since Willie Mays in 1955. Jeff also won his first Silver Slugger Award and was named to his first All-Star team. He won the first Gold Glove Award of his career. **1993** Jeff finished sixth in the league in batting (.320). He missed the final 20 games of the season with a broken bone in his left hand. **1992** Jeff ranked among league leaders in RBIs (sixth, 96) and runs (ninth, 87). **1991** Jeff was the first Houston player to win a Rookie of the Year Award. He led the team in home runs (15), RBIs (82), walks (75), and slugging percentage (.437).

ROBERTO ALOMAR
SECOND BASEMAN, NEW YORK METS

Height 6 feet
Weight 185 lbs.
Birth Date February 5, 1968
Birthplace Ponce, Puerto Rico
Bats Both
Throws Right
Entered Majors 1988

SCOUTING REPORT

Robbie is a fine switch-hitter who can do it all with the bat: hit for power, hit for average, and bunt. He's patient at the plate, often working the count deep and looking for walks to get on base for the big hitters behind him in the lineup. Although Robbie is past his prime as a basestealer, he remains a threat, having stolen 37, 39, and 30 bases from 1999–2001. In the field, Robbie is the best defensive second baseman in the majors, winning 10 Gold Glove Awards in his career. He has great range and a strong throwing arm.

NATIONAL LEGUE

MAJOR LEAGUE CAREER

2001 In Robbie's third season with the Cleveland Indians, he finished third in the A.L. in batting average (.336), fourth in runs scored (113) and sixth in hits (193). He led A.L. second basemen in fielding. Robbie was named to his 12th straight All-Star team, won his 10th Gold Glove Award, and won his fourth Silver Slugger Award. He was signed by the New York Mets before the start of the 2002 season. **2000** Robbie hit over .300 for the eighth time in his career and finished second in the league with 39 stolen bases. He was named to the All-Star Team, and won Golden Glove and Silver Slugger Awards. **1999** In Robbie's first season with the Cleveland Indians, he led the league in runs scored (138). He also picked up his 2,000th career hit on September 22 against the Detroit Tigers' Brian Moehler. He scored the 1,000th run of his career on April 30 against the Texas Rangers. Robbie picked up an All-Star selection, and Gold Glove and Silver Slugger Awards. **1998** In his last season with the Baltimore Orioles, Robbie was named the MVP of the All-Star Game, going three-for-four with a home run, RBI, and stolen base. Robbie also won his seventh Gold Glove. **1997** Robbie suffered through injuries to his ankle, leg, and arm, yet managed to be named to his eighth All-Star team. **1996** Robbie set an Orioles' team record with a then career-high 132 runs scored. He also had a career-high 22-game hitting streak. Robbie was

BASEBALL ALL-STARS

FAST FACTS

> Has won 10 Gold Glove Awards

> Has a .313 batting average in 58 postseason games with four homers and 33 RBIs

> Roberto and his brother, Sandy, Jr., are the only brothers to both be named All-Star Game MVP

named to the All-Star team and won Gold Glove and Silver Slugger Awards. **1995** In his final season with the Toronto Blue Jays, Robbie broke the A.L. record for consecutive games without an error by a second baseman with 104. He was an All-Star for the sixth time and won his fifth Gold Glove. **1994** Robbie made the All-Star team and won a Gold Glove Award. **1993** Robbie finished third in the league in batting with a .326 average. He picked up his 1,000th career hit on August 13 against the Boston Red Sox. He was named to the All-Star team and won a Gold Glove. **1992** Robbie finished third in the league in runs scored (105) and was seventh in batting average (.310). He was an All-Star, and won Gold Glove and Silver Slugger Awards. **1991** In his first season with

Toronto, Robbie finished second in the league in stolen bases (53). He was an All-Star and Gold Glove winner. **1990** In his last season with the San Diego Padres, Robbie was named to his first All-Star team. **1989** In his first full season in the majors, Robbie finished third in the league in hits (184) and was second in stolen bases (42). **1988** Robbie was called up to the Padres after playing nine games in Triple-A in Las Vegas, Nevada. He led San Diego in runs (84) and doubles (24).

PLACIDO POLANCO
THIRD BASEMAN, ST. LOUIS CARDINALS

Height 5 feet 10 inches
Weight 168 lbs.
Birth Date October 10, 1975
Birthplace Santo Domingo, Dominican Republic
Bats Right
Throws Right
Entered Majors 1998

SCOUTING REPORT

Placido is a tough out. Although he doesn't show much power, he makes consistent contact. Placido doesn't draw a lot of walks and will need to show more patience at the plate as he matures. On the bases, he's learning the tricks of becoming a high percentage basestealer and should be good for 15–25 steals in future seasons. Placido is a solid fielder with good range and an accurate throwing arm. He is a versatile player who can play all infield positions and might even see some time in the outfield if the Cards are in a pinch.

FAST FACTS

> Batted .267 in 12 postseason games in 2000 and 2001

> Made only four errors in 144 games in 2001

MAJOR LEAGUE CAREER

2001 Placido batted number two in the Cards' lineup in his first full season as a starter and delivered the numbers St. Louis needed. He finished second on the team in hits (173) and batting average (.307). **2000** Placido's .324 batting average with runners in scoring position was tops on the Cards. He played 51 games at second base, 35 games at third base, and 29 games at shortstop. **1999** Placido spilt the season between St. Louis and Triple-A in Memphis, Tennessee. He batted .301 in games he started with the Cards, batting a sizzling .359 in the month of June. **1998** Placido made his major league debut on July 5, going two-for-four against the Cincinnati Reds. He hit his first major league home run against the Florida Marlins' Rafael Medina.

BASEBALL ALL-STARS

RICH AURILIA
SHORTSTOP, SAN FRANCISCO GIANTS

Height 6 feet 1 inch
Weight 185 lbs.
Birth Date September 2, 1971
Birthplace Brooklyn, New York
Bats Right
Throws Right
Entered Majors 1995

SCOUTING REPORT

Rich really came into his own in 2001, having the best season of his career. He likes to pull the ball, but gets good results when he tries to drive the ball into the leftfield and rightfield gaps. He still needs to show more patience because he has a habit of chasing pitches down and off the plate. On the bases, Rich is not a threat to steal, but he's a smart baserunner who rarely makes mistakes. In the field, Rich has average range and a decent throwing arm.

NATIONAL LEGUE

MAJOR LEAGUE CAREER

2001 Rich had a breakthrough year, establishing himself as the top N.L. shortstop. He led the league in hits (206), becoming only the third Giant to ever reach the 200-hit mark. (Willie Mays had 200 in 1958 and Bobby Bonds had 200 in 1970.) Rich finished sixth in the league in total bases (364) and he led N.L. shortstops in homers and RBIs. He was selected to his first All-Star team and won his first Silver Slugger Award. **2000** Rich led N.L. shortstops in homers (20) and RBIs (79). **1999** Rich led all N.L. shortstops in homers (22). He was also tops among N.L. shortstops in RBIs (78). He had two more RBIs as a pinch hitter in the last game of the season. Rich had more errors than any other major league shortstop (28). **1998** Rich established himself as the Giants' number one shortstop, starting 106 games. He set personal bests at the time in doubles, homers, RBIs, hits, and runs

FAST FACTS

> Slugged MLB's historic first interleague grand slam June 14, 1997, at Anaheim. The bat he used was sent to the Baseball Hall of Fame in Cooperstown, New York.

> Attended St. John's University, in New York City, New York

scored. **1997** Rich was the Giants' reserve shortstop for most of the year. He spent some time at Triple-A in Phoenix, Arizona. All five of his home runs came in a period of only 27 at-bats. **1996** Rich spent almost the full season with the Giants after starting the year at Triple-A in Phoenix, Arizona. He hit 26 points higher after the All-Star break (.248), as opposed to before the break (.222). **1995** Rich saw action in only nine games after playing in Triple-A in Phoenix and Double-A in Shreveport, Louisiana. In his first major league start, he got his first hit, first RBI, and first home run. They came against the Colorado Rockies on September 28.

NATIONAL LEAGUE

SAMMY SOSA
OUTFIELDER, CHICAGO CUBS

Height 6 feet
Weight 220 lbs.
Birth Date November 12, 1968
Birthplace San Pedro De Macoris, Dominican Republic
Bats Right
Throws Right
Entered Majors 1989

SCOUTING REPORT

Sammy's race for the home-run record with Mark McGwire in 1998 made everyone take notice of his hitting ability. Sammy is very strong and he hits to all fields with power. His favorite pitch to hit is anything at his knees. He can knock it out of any ballpark in the league. Sammy has learned to be more selective at the plate, drawing a career-high 116 walks in 2001. In his first few years in the majors, Sammy was a serious basestealing threat, but in recent seasons, he's almost totally stopped trying to steal. He still runs well and is aggressive going for the extra base. In the field, he's got good range and a strong arm.

MAJOR LEAGUE CAREER

2001 Sammy became the first player in major league history to have three 60-home-run seasons. He led the majors in RBIs (160), total bases (425), and runs scored (146). Sammy was named to his fifth All-Star team and won his fifth Silver Slugger Award. **2000** Sammy won his first home-run title, with a major-league leading 50 round-trippers. He won the N.L. Player of the Month for July, after hitting .337 with 11 homers and 24 RBIs in 26 games. Sammy was named to the All-Star team and won the Home Run Derby the day before the All-Star game, in Atlanta, Georgia. He drove in his 1,000th career RBI on June 16. Sammy also won his fourth Silver Slugger Award. **1999** Sammy led the league in total bases (397) and extra-base hits (89). He was the Player of the Month in May, hitting 13 homers with 27 RBIs and 26 runs scored. Sammy was named to his third All-Star team and won his third Silver Slugger Award. **1998** Sammy was named the N.L. MVP, leading the majors in RBIs (158), runs scored (134), and total bases (416). He was named to the All-Star team and won his second Silver Slugger Award. **1997** Sammy got his 1,000th career hit on

NATIONAL LEVEL

FAST FACTS

> Won the N.L. MVP Award in 1998 after hitting 66 homers and leading the majors with 258 RBIs

> The only player in major league history to have three 60-home-run seasons

> Likes to box and watch football

August 20 against the Florida Marlins' Livan Hernandez. He also hit his 200th career homer against Montreal Expo Steve Kline on August 24. **1996** Sammy missed 38 games, due mainly to injuries. He was the N.L. Player of the Month for July, after batting .358 with 10 homers and 29 RBIs in 26 games. **1995** Sammy tied for second in the league in homers with 36. He was named to his first All-Star team and won his first Silver Slugger Award. Sammy also hit the 10,000th home run in Chicago Cubs' history off Los Angeles Dodger Tom Candiotti, on August 14. **1994** Sammy led the Cubs in homers (25), RBIs (70), and batting average (.300). **1993** Sammy became the first player in Cubs' history to have 30 homers and 30 stolen bases in a single season. **1992** In his first season

BASEBALL ALL-STARS

with the Cubs, Sammy was limited to only 67 games, due to injury. **1991** In his final season with the Chicago White Sox, Sammy struggled at the plate, hitting only .203. **1990** In Sammy's first full season in the majors, he was the only player in the A.L. to reach double figures in doubles, triples, homers, and steals. **1989** Sammy split the season between the Texas Rangers (25 games) and Chicago White Sox (33 games). Sammy was traded from the Rangers to the Sox on July 29. He hit his first major league home run off Roger Clemens, then of the Boston Red Sox.

NATIONAL LEAGUE

BARRY BONDS
OUTFIELDER, SAN FRANCISCO GIANTS

Height 6 feet 2 inches
Weight 228 lbs.
Birth Date July 24, 1964
Birthplace Riverside, California
Bats Left
Throws Left
Entered Majors 1986

SCOUTING REPORT

Barry holds the all-time single season home-run record with 73, set in 2001. He has one of the keenest eyes in baseball, drawing a major-league-record 177 walks in the same year. Barry has an uppercut swing that lets him get tremendous height on fly balls hit to the outfield. He remains the best defensive left fielder in the majors, winning eight Gold Gloves.

BASEBALL ALL-STARS

He has a strong, accurate arm and smart baserunners never risk trying to take the the extra base on Barry. He doesn't steal bases as often as he once did, but entering the 2002 season with 484 career steals, he will soon become the only player in baseball history to hit 500 home runs and steal 500 bases. Just when people expected his numbers to tail off because of his age, Barry has, in fact, become an even better ballplayer in his late 30s.

MAJOR LEAGUE CAREER

2001 Barry had one of the greatest seasons in the history of major league baseball. He set the all-time single-season home run record with 73, breaking Mark McGwire's record of 70 set in 1998. Barry also set the major league record for walks in a season with 177. He led the N.L. in slugging percentage (.863, one of the highest of all time) and extra-base hits (107). Barry was named to his 10th All-Star team, won his eighth Gold Glove Award, and won his ninth Silver Slugger Award. He also won his fourth MVP award. **2000** Barry had a sensational season, finishing first in the league in walks (117), second in homers (49) and slugging percentage (.688), tied for third in runs (129), sixth in extra-base hits (81), and 10th in total bases (330). He was named to the All-Star team and won a Silver Slugger Award. **1999** Barry suffered several injuries, which limited him to only 102 games, but he still produced big numbers. He hit 34 homers, marking the 10th straight season in which he's hit over 20 home runs. He got his 2,000th career hit off Atlanta Brave Tom Glavine on September 11. **1998** Barry set a major league record by reaching base in 15 straight appearances at the plate. In that time, he hit two doubles and two homers with five RBIs and six walks. Barry was named to the All-Star team and won a Gold Glove Award. **1997** Barry tied for fourth in the league in homers (40) and ranked second in runs scored (123). He also led the league in walks (145). Barry was named to the All-Star team, won a Gold Glove Award, and won a Silver Slugger Award. **1996** Barry led the league in walks (151) and was second in home runs (42). He became only the second player ever to hit 40 home runs and steal 40 bases in the same season. Barry was N.L. Player of the Month in April, hitting 11 home runs and driving in 32 runs. He was named to the All-Star team, and won Gold Glove and Silver Slugger Awards.

FAST FACTS

> Has won four MVP Awards, more than any other player in major league history

> Has been named to 10 N.L. All-Star teams

> The first major leaguer to steal 400 bases and hit 400 home runs

BASEBALL ALL-STARS

1995 Barry was second in the league in runs scored (109), fourth in homers (33), and sixth in RBIs (104). He also made his fifth All-Star team. **1994** Barry ranked among the N.L. leaders in walks (74, first), homers (37, third), runs (89, fourth), and total bases (253, fifth). He made the All-Star team, and won Gold Glove and Silver Slugger Awards. **1993** In Barry's first season with the Giants, he led the league in homers (46), RBIs (123), and slugging percentage (.677). He was selected the N.L. MVP for the third time. Barry was also named to the All-Star team, and won Gold Glove and Silver Slugger Awards. **1992** In Barry's last season with the Pittsburgh Pirates, he won the N.L. MVP. He led the league in walks (127), runs (109), slugging percentage (.624), and extra-base hits (75). Barry was named the N.L. Player of the Month for April, batting .317 with seven homers and 17 RBIs in 18 games. He won Gold Glove and Silver Slugger Awards. **1991** Barry had another fine season, finishing second in the MVP voting to Terry Pendleton of the Atlanta Braves. Barry won a Gold Glove and Silver Slugger Award. **1990** Barry won his first MVP Award, while becoming only the second player in major league history to hit 30 home runs and steal 50 bases in a single season. (Eric Davis of the Cincinnati Reds did it in 1987.) Barry led the league in slugging percentage (.565). He was named to his first All-Star team and won his first Gold

Glove and Silver Slugger Awards. **1989** Barry finished second in the league with 14 outfield assists. **1988** Barry was named N.L. Player of the Week for April 11–17. **1987** Barry started the season in center field, but was switched to left in late May. **1986** Barry led all N.L. rookies in homers (16), RBIs (48), stolen bases (36), and walks (65).

BASEBALL ALL-STARS

LARRY WALKER
OUTFIELDER, COLORADO ROCKIES

Height 6 feet 3 inches
Weight 235 lbs.
Birth Date December 1, 1966
Birthplace Maple Ridge, British Columbia, Canada
Bats Left
Throws Right
Entered Majors 1989

SCOUTING REPORT

Larry hits the ball to all fields with power and shows great patience at the plate. In the outfield, he's a smart defensive ballplayer with a good arm. He doesn't run as well as he did when he first joined the majors, but he's a smart baserunner who doesn't make foolish mistakes on the basepaths. He posted personal bests in home runs and RBIs in 2001, so there's no reason to believe that he'll be slowing down in the next few seasons.

NATIONAL LEAGUE

MAJOR LEAGUE CAREER

2001 Larry won his third N.L. batting title in four years with a .350 average. At home, in Coors Field, he batted .406 with 20 homers and 74 RBIs. Larry scored his 1,000th career run and stole his 200th career base. He was named to the N.L. All-Star team for the sixth time and won his sixth Gold Glove Award. **2000** Injuries kept Larry limited to only 87 games. Still, he hit .391 with runners in scoring position. He also led the Rockies with 11 outfield assists. **1999** Larry led the league in batting with a .379 average and a .710 slugging percentage. He was named to the All-Star team, won a Gold Glove Award, and won a Silver Slugger Award. **1998** Larry won his first batting title with a .363 average. He won another Gold Glove Award and was again named to the All-Star team. **1997** Larry won the N.L. MVP Award in his best season in the majors. He was the first native Canadian to win a major-league MVP. Larry led the league in homers with 49, was second with a .366 batting average, and third with 130 RBIs. He also led the league with a .720 slugging percentage — the fifth highest in league history. He won a Gold Glove Award, a Silver Slugger Award, and was named to his second All-Star team. Larry was the N.L. Player of the Month in April, hitting 11 homers. **1996** Larry homered in his first at-bat of the season. He knocked in his 500th career RBI on a homer on April 24. **1995** In his first season with the Colorado Rockies, Larry finished second in the league in homers (31), extra-base

BASEBALL ALL-STARS

hits (72), slugging percentage (.607), and total bases (300). **1994** In his final season with the Montreal Expos, Larry played first base for most of the year to ease the strain of a shoulder injury. He tied for the league lead in doubles (44). **1993** Larry won his second Gold Glove and hit his first career grand slam. **1992** Larry earned his first Gold Glove Award, Silver Slugger Award, and was named to his first All-Star team. **1991** Larry had the N.L.'s best second half, batting .338 with 21 doubles, 10 homers, and 41 RBIs after the All-Star break. He played first base for 39 games. **1990** In his first full season in the majors, Larry tied for seventh in Rookie of the Year voting. **1989** Larry made his major league debut on August 16 and got his first career hit off Mike LaCoss of the San Francisco Giants.

FAST FACTS

> Has won three N.L. batting titles in four seasons

> Grew up playing goaltender in hockey and teamed up with Cam Neely, a former All-Star with the Boston Bruins

>> HONORABLE MENTIONS

With so many awesome stars in the major leagues, selecting just 23 as All-Stars is not only tough, it's just not enough. We picked our starting lineups and then looked around.

What about dominating pitchers like Greg Maddux and Roger "the Rocket" Clemens? What about a dynamic duo of shortstops, Derek Jeter and Nomar Garciaparra?

Clearly something had to be done. That something became this Honorable Mentions chapter. We made space for Greg and Roger, for Derek and Nomar. We pitched in another Cy Young–winning pitcher, Tom Glavine, too.

While we were at it, we made space for unhittable closer Billy Wagner. For pop at the plate, we added a pair of outstanding outfielders: Bernie Williams and Shawn Green.

You might feel that some of these talented players shoud be in our starting lineup, instead of the players we picked. That's fine with us. Part of the fun of sports is debating which players are the very best!

BASEBALL ALL-STARS

GREG MADDUX
PITCHER, ATLANTA BRAVES

Height 6 feet
Weight 185 lbs.
Birth Date April 14, 1966
Birthplace San Angelo, Texas
Bats Right
Throws Right
Entered Majors 1986

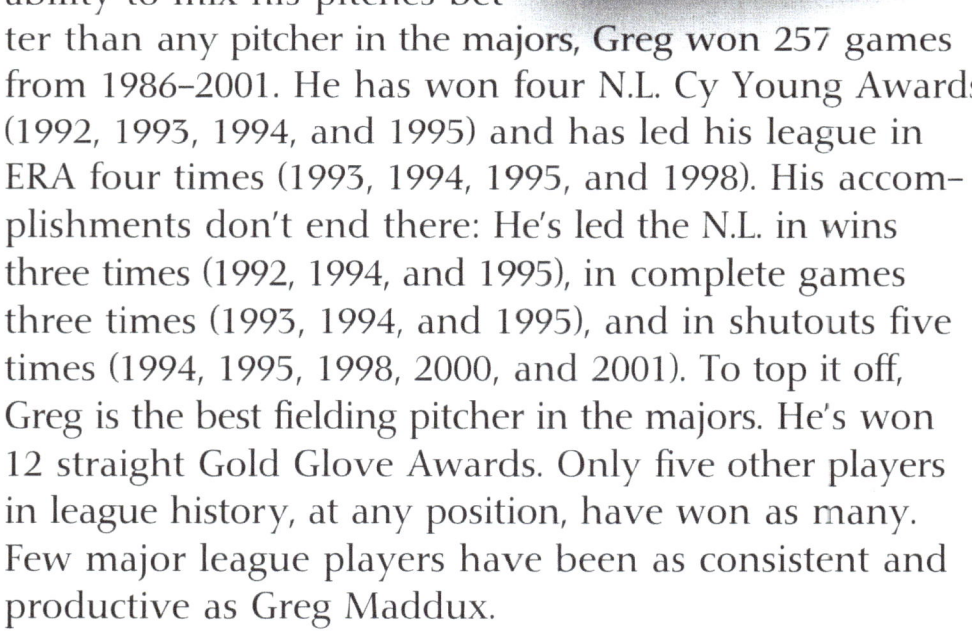

Greg may be the best right-handed pitcher of the 1990s. With pinpoint control and the ability to mix his pitches better than any pitcher in the majors, Greg won 257 games from 1986–2001. He has won four N.L. Cy Young Awards (1992, 1993, 1994, and 1995) and has led his league in ERA four times (1993, 1994, 1995, and 1998). His accomplishments don't end there: He's led the N.L. in wins three times (1992, 1994, and 1995), in complete games three times (1993, 1994, and 1995), and in shutouts five times (1994, 1995, 1998, 2000, and 2001). To top it off, Greg is the best fielding pitcher in the majors. He's won 12 straight Gold Glove Awards. Only five other players in league history, at any position, have won as many. Few major league players have been as consistent and productive as Greg Maddux.

HONORABLE MENTIONS

ROGER CLEMENS
PITCHER, NEW YORK YANKEES

Height 6 feet 4 inches
Weight 235 lbs.
Birth Date August 4, 1962
Birthplace Dayton, Ohio
Bats Right
Throws Right
Entered Majors 1984

Roger is one of the hardest throwers in baseball. Since 1986, he has been leaving batters speechless — and hitless — with his awesome mix of a 97-mile-per-hour fastball, a nasty slider, and a great change-up. Take a look at some of what Roger has accomplished in his career:

- Won six Cy Young Awards — more than anyone in baseball history;

- Led the league in ERA and shutouts six times;

- Led the league in strikeouts five times;

BASEBALL ALL-STARS

- Led the league in wins four times;
- Is 3-0 with a 1.56 ERA in six World Series games, with 43 strikeouts in 40.1 innings.

The doors of baseball's Hall of Fame are wide open — waiting for Roger to take his place among the greatest players of all time.

TOM GLAVINE
PITCHER, ATLANTA BRAVES

Height 6 feet
Weight 185 lbs.
Birth Date March 25, 1966
Birthplace Concord, Massachusetts
Bats Left
Throws Left
Entered Majors 1987

Tom does a great job of mixing his sinking fastball and change-up. He keeps batters off balance by working inside and outside. A fine athlete who fields his position very well, Tom has won at least 13 games in every season from 1991–2001. He won the N.L. Cy Young Award in

HONORABLE MENTIONS

1991 and 1998, and has been named to seven All-Star teams. Tom is a five-time 20-game winner and led the league in wins in each of those seasons (1991, 1992, 1993, 1998, and 2000).

BILLY WAGNER
PITCHER, HOUSTON ASTROS

Height 5 feet 11 inches
Weight 195 lbs.
Birth Date July 25, 1971
Birthplace Tannersville, Virginia
Bats Left
Throws Left
Entered Majors 1995

Billy is one of the shortest pitchers in baseball, but his pitches have been clocked at 100 miles per hour on the radar gun. Mixing his blazing fastball with a nasty slider that freezes N.L. batters cold, Billy is an aggressive dynamo on the mound. He struck out 501 batters in only 343.1 innings from 1995–2001.

During that time, he saved 146 games for the Astros — even though he missed much of the 2000 season with a serious arm injury. Billy was named to the N.L. All-Star team in 1999 and 2001.

DEREK JETER
SHORTSTOP, NEW YORK YANKEES

Height 6 feet 3 inches
Weight 195 lbs.
Birth Date June 26, 1974
Birthplace Pequannock, New Jersey
Bats Right
Throws Right
Entered Majors 1995

It's no coincidence that the New York Yankees have won four world championships since Derek became the team's regular shortstop in 1996. Derek has a .320 batting average from 1995–2001, with 99 homers and 488 RBIs. He has good power to all fields, and is one of the league's best right-handed batters who can drive a pitch

HONORABLE MENTIONS

to right field. He is also one of the league's top percentage basestealers. Derek plays best in big games — he was the World Series MVP in 2000 when he batted .409 with two home runs. He has been named to four All-Star teams, and was named the All-Star Game MVP in 2000. He won the A.L. Rookie of the Year Award in 1996. Derek is regarded by many as the leader of the Yankee team — a role he lives up to season after season.

NOMAR GARCIAPARRA
SHORTSTOP, BOSTON RED SOX

Height 6 feet
Weight 185 lbs.
Birth Date July 23, 1973
Birthplace Whittier, California
Bats Right
Throws Right
Entered Majors 1996

Nomar is one of the new breed of major league shortstops that can hit, hit with power, run, and field like a wizard. (Alex Rodriguez, Derek Jeter, and Miguel Tejada are some of the others.) One of the best fastball hitters in baseball, Nomar won A.L. batting titles in 1999 and 2000 and a Silver Slugger Award in 1997. He also won the A.L. Rookie of the Year Award in 1997, after hitting .306 with 30 homers and 98 RBIs. Nomar has been named to three All-Star teams. In postseason play, he is one of the most feared hitters in the majors. In 13 games, he has batted .383 with seven home runs and 20 RBIs. Injuries limited Nomar to only 21 games in 2001, but no one doubts that he'll be back as one of the league's best all-around performers.

BERNIE WILLIAMS
OUTFIELDER, NEW YORK YANKEES

Height 6 feet 2 inches
Weight 205 lbs.
Birth Date September 13, 1968
Birthplace San Juan, Puerto Rico
Bats Both
Throws Right
Entered Majors 1991

Bernie is the kind of player who can help a team win in many ways. He batted over .300 in seven straight seasons from 1995–2001, winning the A.L. batting title in 1998 with a .339 mark. He has hit

HONORABLE MENTIONS

more than 20 homers in six seasons, and has driven in more than 100 runs in four seasons. He is also a wizard in the field, winning four Gold Glove Awards from 1997–2000. Bernie has been named to four All-Star teams. Since he became the Yankees regular center fielder in 1993, the Yankees have won four world championships (1996, 1998, 1999, and 2000). He's one of baseball's best in big-game situations.

SHAWN GREEN
OUTFIELDER, LOS ANGELES DODGERS

Height 6 feet 4 inches
Weight 200 lbs.
Birth Date November 10, 1972
Birthplace Des Plaines, Illinois
Bats Left
Throws Left
Entered Majors 1993

Shawn is one of the most feared batters in baseball, capable of handling fastballs and curveballs at the plate. He has great power and can drive outside pitches to left field. He's an

BASEBALL ALL-STARS

outstanding defensive player, with a strong and deadly accurate throwing arm. Not too many baserunners try to take an extra base against Shawn. He was named to the 1999 A.L. All-Star team, representing the Toronto Blue Jays. He also won a Gold Glove Award that season. In 2000, he went to the Los Angeles Dodgers. He lit up N.L. pitching in 2001 with 49 homers and 125 RBIs. Shawn is an excellent base stealer — he stole 64 bases in 80 attempts from 1999–2001. Many baseball insiders believe that Shawn's best seasons are still ahead of him.

>> STARS OF THE FUTURE

So far, you've been reading about the very best players of today. But what about tomorrow? Which of baseball's bright young stars will become the All-Stars of the future?

Well, we don't have a crystal ball, but we do watch a lot of players and coaches, and pour over a lot of statistics. Add 'em all up, and you get our seven best guesses. We think these players have the talent, skill, and attitude to become superstars.

Slugger Albert Pujols looks as though he has the swing to start winning batting titles. Alfonso Soriano combines speed and power and has already emerged as one of baseball's top second basemen. Outfielder Lance Berkman has quickly become one of the National League's big bats. Hard-throwing C.C. Sabathia made it big in only his first season in the majors. Mark Mulder has already led his league in wins — in only his second season. Speedy Juan Pierre steals bases by the bunches, and Jimmy Rollins packs power and speed into a small package.

There will be plenty of major league excitement for baseball fans everywhere with these players on the field!

BASEBALL ALL-STARS

ALBERT PUJOLS
OUTFIELDER, ST. LOUIS CARDINALS

Height 6 feet 3 inches
Weight 210 lbs.
Birth Date January 16, 1980
Birthplace Santo Domingo, Dominican Republic
Bats Right
Throws Right
Entered Majors 2001

Albert was an easy choice for the 2001 N.L. Rookie of the Year. He set a league record for RBIs by a rookie (130) and batted .329, ranking him sixth in the N.L. His 194 hits were fifth best in the league and his 360 total bases placed him seventh. Albert not only was a hit at the plate, but he played four different positions (third base, first base, left field, and right field). He was also named to his first All–Star team. Albert is going to be a major league superstar for a long, long time.

STARS OF THE FUTURE

ALFONSO SORIANO
SECOND BASEMAN, NEW YORK YANKEES

Height 6 feet 1 inch
Weight 180 lbs.
Birth Date January 7, 1978
Birthplace San Pedro de Macoris, Dominican Republic
Bats Right
Throws Right
Entered Majors 1999

Alfonso became the Yankees regular second baseman in 2001 and he delivered big time. He is a free swinger who showed plenty of pop with 18 homers. Alfonso led all A.L. rookies in doubles (34), RBIs (73), extra-base hits (55), and homers (18). Equipped with great speed, he finished third in the league in stolen bases (43). In the field, Alfonso has great range, but only an average throwing arm. Still, this young prospect is sure to grow into an even bigger role on the Yankee squad.

BASEBALL ALL-STARS

LANCE BERKMAN
OUTFIELDER, HOUSTON ASTROS

Height 6 feet 1 inch
Weight 220 lbs.
Birth Date February 10, 1976
Birthplace Waco, Texas
Bats Both
Throws Left
Entered Majors 1999

Lance became a regular outfielder with the Astros in the second half of the 2000 season. He quickly showed he could handle big-league pitching, as he clubbed 21 home runs and knocked in 67 runs in only 114 games. In 2001, Lance made it clear that he was one of the league's top rising stars. He was selected to his first All-Star team, while finishing third in the league in batting (.331). He also led the league in doubles (55).

STARS OF THE FUTURE

C.C. SABATHIA
PITCHER, CLEVELAND INDIANS

Height 6 feet 7 inches
Weight 270 lbs.
Birth Date July 21, 1980
Birthplace Vallejo, California
Bats Left
Throws Left
Entered Majors 2001

C.C. (the initials stand for Carsten Charles) made 2001 a rookie year to remember. He led all rookie pitchers in victories (17), starts (33), and strikeouts (171). The hard-throwing lefty has a 96-mile-per-hour fastball to go along with a great curve and change-up.  He mixes his pitches well, keeping batters guessing what he'll be throwing next. For a big man, C.C. fields his position well, especially high bouncers. The Indians are looking for him to continue developing into one of the league's top hurlers.

BASEBALL ALL-STARS

MARK MULDER
PITCHER, OAKLAND ATHLETICS

Height 6 feet 6 inches
Weight 215 lbs.
Birth Date August 5, 1977
Birthplace South Holland, Illinois
Bats Left
Throws Left
Entered Majors 2000

Mark had a disappointing 9–10 rookie season in 2000, but turned things around to establish himself as a top A.L. pitcher in 2001. He led the league with 21 victories and four shutouts. Mark has a great fastball with plenty of movement on it. As part of a tough Oakland pitching staff that boasts Barry Zito and Tim Hudson, Mark finished second in voting for the A.L. Cy Young Award, losing out to the Yankees' Roger Clemens.

STARS OF THE FUTURE

JUAN PIERRE
OUTFIELDER, COLORADO ROCKIES

Height 6 feet
Weight 180 lbs.
Birth Date August 14, 1977
Birthplace Mobile, Alabama
Bats Left
Throws Left
Entered Majors 2000

Juan rose to stardom in 2001, after showing a lot of promise in his rookie season of 2000. In 2001, he batted .327, ninth in the National League. His 46 stolen bases were third highest in the league. His 202 hits and 11 triples were second in the league. Juan is a solid contact hitter who will be making his mark in the majors for a long time.

JIMMY ROLLINS
SHORTSTOP, PHILADELPHIA PHILLIES

Height 5 feet 8 inches
Weight 165 lbs.
Birth Date November 27, 1978
Birthplace Oakland, California
Bats Both
Throws Right
Entered Majors 2000

Jimmy had a great rookie season in 2001, leading the N.L. with 46 stolen bases. Even though he's not a big man, Jimmy's bat can do major damage. He's a line-drive hitter who can go to all fields and has enough pop be a home-run threat. Jimmy is one of the best and fastest baserunners in the league. He gets a good jump when he's stealing a base and he runs aggressively, always looking for the extra base. Jimmy's a solid fielder with an accurate throwing arm. Here's an exciting young player who is only going to get better with time.

≫ TRIBUTES

More than any other sport, baseball is rooted in tradition. Baseball has always celebrated its past while it has moved into the future.

This book has celebrated the brightest stars of today and of tomorrow. Now it's time to take a look at two stars who have already secured a place in baseball history. Cal Ripken, Jr. and Tony Gwynn are not only classy competitors, they are sure-fire Hall of Famers. Both Cal and Tony retired from baseball after the end of the 2001 season.

Cal was a baseball warrior who didn't miss a game for 16 straight seasons. His streak of playing in 2,632 consecutive games ranks among the greatest individual accomplishments in all of sports history.

Tony was the greatest pure hitter of his generation — and one of the greatest of all time. In 1996, he topped the 3,000 career hit mark. Not too many players even get close to that.

Surprisingly, both of these legends spent their entire careers with one team: Cal with the Baltimore Orioles and Tony with the San Diego Padres.

Here is our tribute to two of the game's greatest.

BASEBALL ALL-STARS

CAL RIPKEN, JR.
BALTIMORE ORIOLES 1981 - 2001

Cal is one of only seven players to collect more than 400 home runs and 3,000 hits in a career. (The others are Hank Aaron, Willie Mays, Eddie Murray, Stan Musial, Dave Winfield & Carl Yastrzemski.) He also holds the major league record for home runs hit by a shortstop, with 345. Of course, Cal will forever be remembered by his consecutive playing-game streak of 2,632 games — a record that may never be equaled in major league history.

Cal was A.L. Rookie of the Year in 1982. He was a 19-time All-Star, and won MVP Awards in 1983 and 1991. In his last season in the majors, 2001, Cal won the All-Star Game MVP, highlighted by a dramatic home run. He has been a hero to millions of kids and to many major league stars. He will be missed.

TRIBUTES

TONY GWYNN
SAN DIEGO PADRES 1982 - 2001

Tony was a hitting machine from his rookie season in 1982 until his final season in 2001. He holds the career record for most years leading the N.L. in batting average, with eight. In fact, Tony batted over .300 in the last 19 seasons of his 20-season major league career. He shares the N.L. career record for most years leading the league in hits, with seven. Tony was also selected to 15 All-Star Games and won five Gold Glove Awards. He was one of baseball's most well-liked players of all time. There will never be another one like him.

BASEBALL ALL-STARS

MVP AWARD WINNERS

The Most Valuable Player Award is given to the best major league ballplayer in each league. The first award was given in 1931. Barry Bonds is the only player to win the award more than three times. He has won the MVP four times (1990, 1992, 1993, and 2001).

AMERICAN LEAGUE

YEAR	PLAYER	TEAM	YEAR	PLAYER	TEAM
2001	Ichiro Suzuki	Seattle	1977	Rod Carew	Minnesota
2000	Jason Giambi	Oakland	1976	Thurman Munson	New York
1999	Ivan Rodriguez	Texas	1975	Fred Lynn	Boston
1998	Juan Gonzalez	Texas	1974	Jeff Burroughs	Texas
1997	Ken Griffey, Jr.	Seattle	1973	Reggie Jackson	Oakland
1996	Juan Gonzalez	Texas	1972	Dick Allen	Chicago
1995	Mo Vaughn	Boston	1971	Vida Blue	Oakland
1994	Frank Thomas	Chicago	1970	Boog Powell	Baltimore
1993	Frank Thomas	Chicago	1969	Harmon Killebrew	Minnesota
1992	Dennis Eckersley	Oakland	1968	Denny McLain	Detroit
1991	Cal Ripken, Jr.	Baltimore	1967	Carl Yastrzemski	Boston
1990	Rickey Henderson	Oakland	1966	Frank Robinson	Baltimore
1989	Robin Yount	Milwaukee	1965	Zoilo Versalles	Minnesota
1988	Jose Canseco	Oakland	1964	Brooks Robinson	Baltimore
1987	George Bell	Toronto	1963	Elston Howard	New York
1986	Roger Clemens	Boston	1962	Mickey Mantle	New York
1985	Don Mattingly	New York	1961	Roger Maris	New York
1984	Willie Hernandez	Detroit	1960	Roger Maris	New York
1983	Cal Ripken, Jr.	Baltimore	1959	Nellie Fox	Chicago
1982	Robin Yount	Milwaukee	1958	Jackie Jensen	Boston
1981	Rollie Fingers	Milwaukee	1957	Mickey Mantle	New York
1980	George Brett	Kansas City	1956	Mickey Mantle	New York
1979	Don Baylor	California	1955	Yogi Berra	New York
1978	Jim Rice	Boston	1954	Yogi Berra	New York

AMERICAN LEAGUE (CONTINUED)

YEAR	PLAYER	TEAM
1953	Al Rosen	Cleveland
1952	Bobby Shantz	Philadelphia
1951	Yogi Berra	New York
1950	Phil Rizzuto	New York
1949	Ted Williams	Boston
1948	Lou Boudreau	Cleveland
1947	Joe DiMaggio	New York
1946	Ted Williams	Boston
1945	Hal Newhouser	Detroit
1944	Hal Newhouser	Detroit
1943	Spud Chandler	New York
1942	Joe Gordon	New York
1941	Joe DiMaggio	New York
1940	Hank Greenberg	Detroit
1939	Joe DiMaggio	New York
1938	Jimmie Foxx	Boston
1937	Charlie Gehringer	Detroit
1936	Lou Gehrig	New York
1935	Hank Greenberg	Detroit
1934	Mickey Cochrane	Detroit
1933	Jimmie Foxx	Philadelphia
1932	Jimmie Foxx	Philadelphia
1931	Lefty Grove	Philadelphia

NATIONAL LEAGUE

YEAR	PLAYER	TEAM
2001	Barry Bonds	San Francisco
2000	Jeff Kent	San Francisco
1999	Chipper Jones	Atlanta
1998	Sammy Sosa	Chicago
1997	Larry Walker	Colorado
1996	Ken Caminiti	San Diego
1995	Barry Larkin	Cincinnati
1994	Jeff Bagwell	Houston
1993	Barry Bonds	San Francisco
1992	Barry Bonds	Pittsburgh
1991	Terry Pendleton	Atlanta
1990	Barry Bonds	Pittsburgh
1989	Kevin Mitchell	San Francisco
1988	Kirk Gibson	Los Angeles
1987	Andre Dawson	Chicago
1986	Mike Schmidt	Philadelphia
1985	Willie McGee	St. Louis
1984	Ryne Sandberg	Chicago
1983	Dale Murphy	Atlanta
1982	Dale Murphy	Atlanta
1981	Mike Schmidt	Philadelphia
1980	Mike Schmidt	Philadelphia
1979	Keith Hernandez	St. Louis
	Willie Stargell	Pittsburgh
1978	Dave Parker	Pittsburgh
1977	George Foster	Cincinnati
1976	Joe Morgan	Cincinnati
1975	Joe Morgan	Cincinnati
1974	Steve Garvey	Los Angeles
1973	Pete Rose	Cincinnati
1972	Johnny Bench	Cincinnati
1971	Joe Torre	St. Louis
1970	Johnny Bench	Cincinnati
1969	Willie McCovey	San Francisco

BASEBALL ALL-STARS

NATIONAL LEAGUE (CONTINUED)

YEAR	PLAYER	TEAM	YEAR	PLAYER	TEAM
1968	Bob Gibson	St. Louis	1949	Jackie Robinson	Brooklyn
1967	Orlando Cepeda	St. Louis	1948	Stan Musial	St. Louis
1966	Roberto Clemente	Pittsburgh	1947	Bob Elliott	Boston
1965	Willie Mays	San Francisco	1946	Stan Musial	St. Louis
1964	Ken Boyer	St. Louis	1945	Phil Cavarretta	Chicago
1963	Sandy Koufax	Los Angeles	1944	Marty Marion	St. Louis
1962	Maury Wills	Los Angeles	1943	Stan Musial	St. Louis
1961	Frank Robinson	Cincinnati	1942	Mort Cooper	St. Louis
1960	Dick Groat	Pittsburgh	1941	Dolph Camilli	Brooklyn
1959	Ernie Banks	Chicago	1940	Frank McCormick	Cincinnati
1958	Ernie Banks	Chicago	1939	Bucky Walters	Cincinnati
1957	Hank Aaron	Milwaukee	1938	Ernie Lombardi	Cincinnati
1956	Don Newcombe	Brooklyn	1937	Joe Medwick	St. Louis
1955	Roy Campanella	Brooklyn	1936	Carl Hubbell	New York
1954	Willie Mays	New York	1935	Gabby Hartnett	Chicago
1953	Roy Campanella	Brooklyn	1934	Dizzy Dean	St. Louis
1952	Hank Sauer	Chicago	1933	Carl Hubbell	New York
1951	Roy Campanella	Brooklyn	1932	Chuck Klein	Philadelphia
1950	Jim Konstanty	Philadelphia	1931	Frankie Frisch	St. Louis

ROOKIE OF THE YEAR AWARD WINNERS

Each season, one outstanding rookie is named Rookie of the Year in each league. In 1947 and 1948, only one Rookie of the Year Award was given. Jackie Robinson was the first winner of the award. Since 1949, each league has selected its own Rookie of the Year.

AMERICAN LEAGUE

YEAR	PLAYER	TEAM	YEAR	PLAYER	TEAM
2001	Ichiro Suzuki	Seattle	1977	Eddie Murray	Baltimore
2000	Kazuhiro Sasaki	Seattle	1976	Mark Fidrych	Detroit
1999	Carlos Beltran	Kansas City	1975	Fred Lynn	Boston
1998	Ben Grieve	Oakland	1974	Mike Hargrove	Texas
1997	Nomar Garciaparra	Boston	1973	Al Bumbry	Baltimore
1996	Derek Jeter	New York	1972	Carlton Fisk	Boston
1995	Marty Cordova	Minnesota	1971	Chris Chambliss	Cleveland
1994	Bob Hamelin	Kansas City	1970	Thurman Munson	New York
1993	Tim Salmon	California	1969	Lou Piniella	Kansas City
1992	Pat Listach	Milwaukee	1968	Stan Bahnsen	New York
1991	Chuck Knoblauch	Minnesota	1967	Rod Carew	Minnesota
1990	Sandy Alomar, Jr.	Cleveland	1966	Tommie Agee	Chicago
1989	Gregg Olson	Baltimore	1965	Curt Blefary	Baltimore
1988	Walt Weiss	Oakland	1964	Tony Oliva	Minnesota
1987	Mark McGwire	Oakland	1963	Gary Peters	Chicago
1986	Jose Canseco	Oakland	1962	Tom Tresh	New York
1985	Ozzie Guillen	Chicago	1961	Don Schwall	Boston
1984	Alvin Davis	Seattle	1960	Ron Hansen	Baltimore
1983	Ron Kittle	Chicago	1959	Bob Allison	Washington
1982	Cal Ripken, Jr.	Baltimore	1958	Albie Pearson	Washington
1981	Dave Righetti	New York	1957	Tony Kubek	New York
1980	Joe Charboneau	Cleveland	1956	Luis Aparicio	Chicago
1979	John Castino	Minnesota	1955	Herb Score	Cleveland
	Alfredo Griffin	Toronto	1954	Bob Grim	New York
1978	Lou Whitaker	Detroit	1953	Harvey Kuenn	Detroit

BASEBALL ALL-STARS

AMERICAN LEAGUE (CONTINUED)

YEAR	PLAYER	TEAM	YEAR	PLAYER	TEAM
1952	Harry Byrd	Philadelphia	1949	Roy Sievers	St. Louis Browns
1951	Gil McDougald	New York	1948	Alvin Dark	Boston (NL)
1950	Walt Dropo	Boston	1947	Jackie Robinson	Brooklyn (NL)

NATIONAL LEAGUE

YEAR	PLAYER	TEAM	YEAR	PLAYER	TEAM
2001	Albert Pujols	St. Louis	1975	John Montefusco	San Francisco
2000	Rafael Furcal	Atlanta	1974	Bake McBride	St. Louis
1999	Scott Williamson	Cincinnati	1973	Gary Matthews	San Francisco
1998	Kerry Wood	Chicago	1972	Jon Matlack	New York
1997	Scott Rolen	Philadelphia	1971	Earl Williams	Atlanta
1996	Todd Hollandsworth	Los Angeles	1970	Carl Morton	Montreal
1995	Hideo Nomo	Los Angeles	1969	Ted Sizemore	Los Angeles
1994	Raul Mondesi	Los Angeles	1968	Johnny Bench	Cincinnati
1993	Mike Piazza	Los Angeles	1967	Tom Seaver	New York
1992	Eric Karros	Los Angeles	1966	Tommy Helms	Cincinnati
1991	Jeff Bagwell	Houston	1965	Jim Lefebvre	Los Angeles
1990	Dave Justice	Atlanta	1964	Dick Allen	Philadelphia
1989	Jerome Walton	Chicago	1963	Pete Rose	Cincinnati
1988	Chris Sabo	Cincinnati	1962	Ken Hubbs	Chicago
1987	Benito Santiago	San Diego	1961	Billy Williams	Chicago
1986	Todd Worrell	St. Louis	1960	Frank Howard	Los Angeles
1985	Vince Coleman	St. Louis	1959	Willie McCovey	San Francisco
1984	Dwight Gooden	New York	1958	Orlando Cepeda	San Francisco
1983	Darryl Strawberry	New York	1957	Jack Sanford	Philadelphia
1982	Steve Sax	Los Angeles	1956	Frank Robinson	Cincinnati
1981	Fernando Valenzuela	Los Angeles	1955	Bill Virdon	St. Louis
1980	Steve Howe	Los Angeles	1954	Wally Moon	St. Louis
1979	Rick Sutcliffe	Los Angeles	1953	Jim Gilliam	Brooklyn
1978	Bob Horner	Atlanta	1952	Joe Black	Brooklyn
1977	Andre Dawson	Montreal	1951	Willie Mays	New York
1976	Butch Metzger	San Diego	1950	Sam Jethroe	Boston
	Pat Zachry	Cincinnati	1949	Don Newcombe	Brooklyn

>> GLOSSARY

Cy Young Award an annual honor given to the best pitcher in each major league

Earned run average (ERA) the average number of runs a pitcher allows every nine innings

Gold Glove Award an annual honor given to the best fielding player at each position in each major league

premier the best or earliest at doing something

Silver Slugger Award an annual honor given to the best-hitting player at each position in each major league

unanimously when something is done by two or more people who agree completely

RESOURCES

Christopher, Matt. *On the Field with Alex Rodriguez.* New York, NY: Little Brown & Company, 2002.

Grant, Evan, and Bob Rains (editor). *Juan Gonzalez: Juan Gone!* Champaign, IL: Sports Publishing, 1999.

Kernan, Kevin. *Bernie Williams: Quiet Superstar.* New York, NY: Econo-Clad Books, 1999.

Savage, Jeff. *Barry Bonds: Record Breaker.* Minneapolis, MN: Lerner Publishings, 2002.

Stone, Larry, and Bob Rains (editor). *Randy Johnson: Arizona Heat!* Champaign, IL: Sports Publishing, 1999.

>> RESOURCES

MAGAZINE
Sports Illustrated for Kids
135 West 50th Street
New York, NY 10020
(800) 992-0196
http://www.sikids.com

WEB SITES
Sports Illustrated for Kids
http://www.sikids.com
Check out the latest sports news, cool games, and much more.

The Official Site of Major League Baseball
http://www.mlb.com

RESOURCES

The following sites offer complete coverage of baseball action:

http://sportsillustrated.cnn.com/baseball

http://www.sports.espn.go.com/mlb/index

http://www.sports.yahoo.com/mlb

For stats and complete historical coverage of baseball, try these sites:

http://www.baseball-reference.com

http://www.baseball-almanac.com

INDEX

accurate, 33, 64, 74, 90, 98
assortment, 8
authority, 39

Baseball Hall of Fame, 24

Canseco, Jose, 29
change-up, 8, 12, 51, 83–84, 95
conditioning, 44
consecutive, 18, 62, 99–100
criticism, 31
curveballs, 12, 89
Cy Young Award, 9–10, 45, 48–49, 52, 84, 96

debut, 13, 22, 25, 30, 50, 56

earned run average, 9

Fenway Park, 9, 36
fielding percentage, 24–25, 27

Gold Glove Award, 24, 32, 59, 61–62, 74–75, 79–80, 90
grand slam, 58, 80

Home Run Derby, 70

Japan, 10

Mays, Willie, 59, 67, 100

on-base percentage, 21, 41
overhand, 12, 44

>> INDEX

premier, 26

reinterpretation, 14
reserve, 68
Robinson, Jackie, 32
rotator cuff, 9

save percentage, 15
Silver Slugger Award, 19, 21, 24, 29–30, 34, 37, 40–41, 55–56, 58, 61–62, 67, 70–71, 74–76, 79–80, 88
slider, 8, 44, 47, 83, 85
slugging percentage, 17, 21, 24, 34, 55, 58–59, 74, 76, 79, 80
strike zone, 14, 17

Thornton, Andre, 37
Triple Crown, 28

unanimously, 9
unique, 31

velocity, 9
versatile, 64
veteran, 4–5

World Series, 4, 14–15, 24, 45, 48, 55, 84, 87